TRUST THE PROCESS:

Reap The Harvest

Visionary: Dr. Mary J. Huntley

Foreword: Dr. Jennifer Jones Bryant

© 2024 by Dr. Mary J. Huntley

ISBN: 979-8-218-45711-2

Cover Design By: Mr. Vincent Dadzie

Published By: Dr. Mary J. Huntley

FULFILLMENT

As defined in the Oxford Dictionary, fulfillment is the achievement of something desired, promised, or predicted.

The first four authors will share their awesome stories with themes centered around fulfillment and purpose. Some of their favorite scriptures are listed below.

Jeremiah 29:11 "For I know the thoughts that I think toward you, says the Lord, thoughts of peace and not of evil, to give you a future and a hope." (NKJV)

Jeremiah 29:11 "For I know the plans I have for you," says the LORD, "They are plans for good and not for disaster, to give you a future and a hope." (New Living Translation)

Proverbs 19:21 "There are many devices in a man's heart; nevertheless the counsel of the LORD, that shall stand." (KJV)

Eccles. 3:1 "To everything there is a season, and a time to every purpose under the heaven." (KJV)

ENDORSEMENTS

*T*rust *The Process: Reap the Harvest* is the phenomenal unveiling of the latest literary gem whose one-word description is transformative. Life is a series of strategic processes, whether you're choosing a college, a spouse, a job, or a house. Allow Visionary Dr. Mary J. Huntley and her amazing co-authors to show you the way. They have done a remarkable job sharing invaluable wisdom and tips to help us trust the process and reap God's harvest in due season. I was honored and blessed to host Dr. Mary and her co-authors on my *Powerless to Powerful* podcast. Their compelling and powerful narratives left Australia enriched and empowered, and their unwavering commitment to live out the book's title resonates unequivocally. This book is a must-read!

Dr. Angela Bennett, Australia

Angie B. Transformations

"A book filled with encouragement for anyone struggling with life's difficulties. I myself, like everyone, experience life's ups and downs. This book helped me look and trust God's whole plan for me."

Abhijit Ganguly, CEO
UP WORDS Magazine, India

ENDORSEMENTS

Trust the Process: Reap the Harvest is an anthology compiled by Dr. Mary J. Huntley, consisting of 9 great co-authors (Dr. Jennifer Jones Bryant (Executive Strategic Advisor/Foreword Author), Dr. Rhonda M. Wood (Featured Author), Dr. Theresa A. Moseley, Dr. Talvia Peterson, Nadia Monsano, Nicole Gwanzura, MBA (Executive Administrator), LaTrish Thomas, Dennika Davenport, and Michelle Hammond who shared their life's stumbling blocks as stepping stones. This book is powerful, packed with stories of victories resulting from God's process during challenges and reaping successful harvests.

Trust the Process: Reap the Harvest is a book that is needed in such a time as now. It is a timeless, valuable book that can be used to guide an individual to embrace uncertainty, challenges, and cultivate resilience. Readers will appreciate the thought-provoking insights which will encourage them to release the grip of anxiety and impatience while leaning into the ebb and flow of life's rhythm. I highly recommend *Trust the Process: Reap the Harvest.*

Dr. Kishma A. George,
Editor-In-Chief/CEO
K.I.S.H.® Magazine

This groundbreaking anthology isn't just a book, it's a roadmap to help identify and embrace how to unlock the possibilities of success, abundance, and fulfillment in every aspect of your life. Visionary Dr. Mary J. Huntley has gathered information, the support of, and collaborated with other amazing leaders to pen and compile this extraordinary guide. This award-winning collection illuminates the path to victory, inspiring readers to embrace trust, perseverance, and growth. Each page is a testament to the power of resilience and belief in the process, promising a bountiful harvest of success and fulfillment; through practical strategies to guide you towards purpose and prosperity, that promises to revolutionize your journey towards an abundant life. Embark on an extraordinary journey of transformation with "Trust the Process, Reap the Harvest: Your Blueprint for Victorious Living."

Discover the following: Proven practices, principles, and techniques for overcoming obstacles and embracing challenges, turning setbacks into stepping stones, and transcending limitations to achieve greatness with resilience and grace. Inspiring real-life stories of individuals who have harnessed the power of trust to transform adversity into triumph. Actionable steps to ignite your inner potential, unleash your creativity, cultivate a mindset of abundance, and unlock the doors of unlimited possibilities. This page-turner offers a beacon of hope and a catalyst for positive change. A comprehensive guide to help you navigate life's twists and turns with confidence and clarity. Take the first step towards your brightest future today with *Trust the Process, Reap the Harvest*. Read it with a friend, and start a book club to empower others while you are on your journey. You will be glad that you did!

Dr. Angela Seay,
Elite Ms. North Carolina Petite 2024,
Your Favorite Holistic Wellness Practitioner
Health Educator, with D3 Health Fitness, LLC

DEDICATION

This book is dedicated to:

Dr. Ronald Lee Huntley, my amazingly supportive husband of 50 years. You are the love of my life next to my Lord and Savior Jesus Christ. I am honored to be your wife and I love you very much. THANK YOU for your unwavering support, and your endless, unconditional love.

Kelvin J. Massie, my awesome son. Thank you for your love, prayers, and support during my many endeavors. I love you to life. Continue to trust the process, knowing that you will surely reap an overwhelmingly successful harvest.

My mom, **Mrs. Carrie Lee Edwards**, THANK YOU for leaving me a rich legacy of faith in God and fervent prayer. Thank you for regularly taking me to church at a very early age to ensure that I was spiritually grounded. Thank you for every sacrifice you made for me as a single mom. I am eternally grateful.

The loving memory of my grandmother, **Mrs. Carrie James,** THANK YOU for accepting and receiving me when I was discharged from the hospital after birth. Thank you for allowing me to rest in your arms surrounded by your genuine love. THANK YOU for welcoming me into your home once again when my mom and I moved to Washington, DC. You took precious time to nurture me during the years. Thank you for relinquishing a job to me to ensure that I would earn money to support myself. THANK YOU for a rich legacy of faith in God, love, awesome work ethic, and integrity. I am so grateful for every sacrifice you made so that I could realize my dreams. It was an honor to be in your room while you transitioned to be with the Lord.

My siblings, **Barbara, Calvin, and Ronnie,** I love you to the moon and back, and then some more. Thanks for sharing my journey.

Cousin, **Sgt. Cornell James,** I love you, and I am honored to call you "Cuz."

The loving memory of **Mrs. Bertha Lee Huntley,** THE BEST mother-in-love in the world.   THANK YOU for your unconditional love. You always treated me as your biological daughter. You always made me feel loved and appreciated. You were always in my "front row" to cheer for me and to celebrate my accomplishments.

The loving memory of my cousin **Specialist E4 Kenneth James, 8-year military veteran,** I am so honored to have been a part of your life.

ACKNOWLEDGEMENTS

I thank GOD for the vision and the faith to serve as the Visionary of HIS assignment. Thank you for finally releasing me to write and publish this masterpiece to bring you glory in the name of our Lord Jesus. I trusted the process and waited until you said, "Now is the time." And of course, you allowed all of the pieces to come together. You sent destiny helpers to ensure that this vision would manifest while globally impacting the world. Thank you for choosing me as the vessel to motivate, educate, and activate your daughters to become first-time international bestselling authors; and to unleash their untapped potential. Serving as the Project Visionary has allowed me to become a stronger, wiser, and more determined servant. Interestingly enough, you gave me the manuscript for *Don't Quit, my international* bestseller. Now you encouraged me to *Trust The Process: Reap The Harvest.* Thank you, God. I did my best to bring YOU ALL the glory! I am honored that you chose me for this assignment!

I am ecstatically grateful for an amazing professional graphic designer, Mr. Vincent Dadzie. Thank you for collaborating with me, and for your creative, phenomenal gift of my awesome Trust The Process: Reap The Harvest book cover. Your professionalism, patience, and creativity are appreciated beyond what I am able to articulate. Your willingness to avail yourself and accommodate my schedule is commendable and greatly appreciated. You are the epitome of the amazingly good individuals in the world. Thank you for capturing my vision and helping me to share it with the readers. Your awesome depiction of a beautiful, ripe wheat field represents an overwhelmingly successful harvest, and your depiction of the clouds in the background on the front cover holds symbolism of hope, guidance, and divine presence. Just as clouds provide shade, relief, and a sense of hope, they also represent a guiding force through challenges, aligning with the theme of embracing uncertainty while reaping the rewards of trust. You have allowed the readers to envision my vision for this awesome anthology, THANK YOU VERY MUCH!

Thank you to my Trust the Process executive team, Dr. Jennifer Jones Bryant, Nicole Gwanzura, and Nadia Monsano. I'm extremely grateful for my awesome endorsers, Dr. Angela Bennett, Dr. Kishma George, Dr. Angela Seay, and Abhijit Ganguly, who offered an immediate and resounding "YES." I could not have completed this amazing anthology without GOD, my industry experts, co-authors, prayer warriors, and mentors. THANK YOU ALL, I APPRECIATE YOUR SUPPORT!

**Dr. Mary J. Huntley,
Ph.D., D. Min.**

A VERY SPECIAL DEDICATION
TO OUR VIP SUPPORTERS

THANK YOU, our amazing supporters. You are greatly appreciated!

Dr. Angela Bennett
Dr. Angela Seay
Dr. Kimberly Dixon Carroll
Dr. Ronald Lee Huntley
Brenda Joyce Thomas
Marcia Elaine Huntley
Tonya Yvette Huntley
Dr. Kishma George
Kelvin J. Massie
Abhijit Ganguly
Dr. Patricia Gilchrist
Dr. Sharon Sauls
Kathy Mouton
Candace Forcer
Clyde Forcer
Marieca Murphy
Quineice Sheppard
Vernon Giscombe
Serena Johnson
Elana Toliver
Georgina Motley
Wilberto Castro
Temeecka Tillison
Dominique Manigault
Mary Jackson
Simone Carroll
Ann Paxson
Thanhha Nguyen
Karen Jenkins
David Reid
Gwendolyn Simon

Gwendolyn Gayden
Valerie January
Dorine Rascoe
Mary Maczko
Charles Wilder
Julie Hedrick
Sandy Bakar
Belinda Lewis
Ericka Parker
Anita Willingham
Davlyn Jagdeo
Tehani Matthews
Tamika Webb
Cheryl Mazique
Lionel Scatliffe
Sofia Frazier
Antoinette Cannady
Robin White
Demtricia McCall
Jamicka Edwards
Aaron Spurling
Beverly Walker
Jeffrey Brown
Steven Shulse
Rashunda Taylor
Anthony Gunter
Mary Cunningham
Alonda Brooks
Mary Cary
Jeannell Graham
Brittany Osborne
Nichole Moraldo
Linda Bourgeois
Ingrid Thomas

TABLE OF CONTENTS

INTRODUCTION

"Trust in the Lord with all your heart, and lean not on your own understanding. In all your ways acknowledge Him, and He will make your paths straight." Proverbs 3:5-6

Have you noticed that life involves a series of processes? Whether you're choosing a college, spouse, job, or house, your decision requires executing a strategic process. You must trust the process and wait for it to yield your realistic expectation or overwhelmingly successful harvest. And yes, the wait can seem to wear you down. However, when you shift your mindset to the outcome, the wait becomes easier. I vividly recall the American dream many of us have experienced. I wanted to become a homeowner. However, I had to wait until all the requirements were met before it came to fruition. The loan process required strategic steps to ensure my creditworthiness. I secured the proper job to receive adequate compensation for the payment of necessary bills and financial obligations in a timely manner. Paying on time ensured proper credit reporting scores that greatly impacted the mortgage process. My finances with the banking institution required certain minimal balances to show responsible spending. Once I met the lending institution's criteria, I was able to secure the loan to purchase my dream home; but not before several scary tactics tried to pull me off course (abort the process). Mistakenly, another contract was connected to my dream property. At closing, another scare tactic appeared that caused my realtor to reschedule closing to the next day. While I was greatly disappointed, I continued to trust the process and not waver. This was not the easiest loan process but because it was the best way to secure what I needed, I trusted the process and reaped an overwhelmingly successful harvest including retiring my mortgage six years earlier.

Have you ever wondered what it took for you to experience the amazing cup of coffee you enjoy? I paraphrased Pastor Keith

Battle's awesome story about processing coffee beans to illustrate a point. "Before it became your favorite coffee, it started out as coffee beans that were planted in a dark place. When the seeds were harvested, they had to be dried, and then roasted in temperatures that exceeded 500 degrees Fahrenheit. Those coffee beans had to be pulverized in a grinder literally changing the composition of each bean. And if that wasn't enough after going through a grinder, that ground-roasted coffee would then have to be boiled and brewed in boiling hot water. WHAT A PROCESS!" It had to go through all of that to become what you enjoy today. You see, sometimes we look at successful people and where they are. But we have no clue what they went through to get there–the dark places, the grinding, the crushing. The things that broke them down to difficulties that they went through. And sometimes we think we want what they have. But that's because just like that coffee we caught a whiff and fragrance of their success. But we have no idea what it took for them to get there.

In essence, we see their glory without knowing their authentic story, sleepless nights, heartaches, pain, and numerous setbacks. However, they refused to give up until they were declared the winner by unanimous decision. They patted themselves on the back, cheered for themselves, persevered through the pain, triumphed through tears, and marched through mayhem. That is how they reaped an overwhelmingly successful harvest, and we must do the same. Become your best cheerleader during the process!

I am blessed to have garnered support from some of the most amazing women of color, and star-studded industry experts for this amazing anthology compilation. Though we are qualified, competent, and confident it is no secret that women are still challenged with having to break the glass ceiling in their careers. It is no secret that we still earn less than our male counterparts. We continue to overcome various discriminatory practices as we show up with integrity and excellence. I remember very vividly when Judge Ketanji Brown Jackson made history as she became the first Black female Supreme Court Justice on June 30, 2022. Finally, through much controversy, a woman of color had the opportunity to take a well-deserved seat among the other justices. If you have ever been challenged with breaking the glass ceiling in a position, you are not alone. One author shares her victorious story of trusting the process after hitting the glass ceiling. She has since become an international speaker, global award recipient, world-famous M.C., and multi-award winner including the Presidential Lifetime Achievement Award. Step by step, she trusts the process and receives overwhelmingly successful harvests.

Another phenomenal bilingual author shares her educational quest after making America her new home. Would she become acclimated to her new neighborhood and new school? There were so many unanswered questions. However, she began her new journey. Eventually, she enrolled in the master's program at her preferred university. She met new friends, found a job, and did very well. But school and work eventually caused her to be placed on academic probation. What would she do? What would her parents say? Would she graduate on time? You must read this encouraging story to see how she trusted the process and received an overwhelmingly successful harvest.

Yet another awesome author shares her story of trusting the process to overcome homelessness. This was not an easy feat. However, she did not give up let alone give in. She persevered through the challenges because she knew that she could and would eventually do better. She found her tribe and continued to receive and provide mutual support until the tables turned. She continued to hone her skills and trust the process. She never lost hope because she knew that her situation would soon pass. As a result, she began to seize the moments and, in her chapter, shares the tips she used to overcome the challenges she faced.

Another author tells her painful and challenging account of rejection by someone she loved. She addresses salient questions such as, "Am I worthy. Am I deserving. Am I attractive?" and a few others after allowing self-doubt to creep in. She later shares how rejection can sometimes be God's protection. WOW, did you ever perceive rejection from that perspective? As you read further into the chapters by these remarkable authors, you'll have the opportunity to glean impactful wisdom and knowledge from their compelling and transformative stories, as well as the awesome tips they share.

When you are planted in a dark place and feel forgotten, overlooked, or unnoticed; keep shining. God knows exactly where you are and how long you should be there. He knows what it takes to build faith, stability, tenacity, and endurance. Keep shining and before long you will notice that some things that pulled you off course earlier in life, have now become funny. You will recognize that they are no longer a distraction. Keep shining so that others who are planted in your area will be able to see your light and make it to safety. Keep shining until you eventually realize that this was all factored into your growth process. While the discomfort of growth pains hurt, they also help. So, trust the process and don't dare attempt to abort it. If you attempt to abort it, you will surely come up short. You will miss the growth opportunities that include character development, patience, experience, and several important life lessons. Trust the process that will enable you to share your lessons with those assigned to you during your journey. Allow them to glean hope knowing that you survived the same challenge they're facing. Remember that while your story is about you, it is not for you. Your story allows you to empower, educate, and equip others to press into adversity until their stumbling blocks become stepping stones to victory.

Though your process may have seemed long, drawn out, and unobtainable, when you get to the end you will not look like what you've been through. It may have felt like a fiery furnace, but you will not smell like smoke. Lastly, to those who may be experiencing a challenging situation or circumstance … trust the process. Do not sabotage yourself by attempting to abort the process or your destiny. Fasten your seatbelt and prepare for your victorious journey ahead.

TRUST THE PROCESS

By Dr. Mary J. Huntley

Trust the process, though it may seem to lead to many paths,
Some paths may be familiar, others are provided
to keep you on task.
Trust the process that will soon become your very close friend,
So, embrace its many facets and you'll understand it in the end.
Trust the process, that will BUILD character and courage,
Though many times while trusting you may become discouraged.

Trust this much-needed, life-changing
valuable process, exclusively designed for YOU,
In the end, you will see that it allowed you to get through.
You'll look back in awe and see how far you've come,
You successfully navigated the challenges, and indeed
YOU DID overcome.
So, continue to trust the process, though you don't
know every detail.
But in your heart of hearts YOU KNOW, you'll reap an abundant
harvest WITHOUT FAIL!

Trust the process, when it seems no strength is left,
Press on step by step, just be sure to give your best.
Trust the process when others may not understand,
Believe in yourself, encourage yourself, tell yourself,
"YES, I CAN."
So don't you dare consider quitting no matter how hard it gets,
Trust the process, run YOUR race, stay the course 'cause
you ain't seen nothing yet!
VICTORY IS IN YOUR DNA! LET'S GOOO!

SEVEN STEPS THAT LEAD TO A VICTORIOUS PROCESS AND AN AWESOMELY ABUNDANT HARVEST

Persist in the face of adversity. This is probably not your first rodeo, so let's do this!

Resist the urge to abort. Do not sabotage yourself!

Onward, only look ahead. That is the only direction that's important!

Continue, laser-focused on your goal!

Expect to win while trusting the process. Your abundant harvest awaits!

Soar above negativity because it will not produce your goal!

Success shall be your portion if you stay the course!

Dr. Mary J. Huntley serves as a servant leader in her 50l (c)(3) organization. She is an Official Presenter of the Presidential Lifetime Achievement as well as a recipient of this prestigious award. She is the blessed and grateful recipient of earned Doctor of Philosophy and Doctor of Ministry Degrees. She holds various titles and serves in several capacities including CEO, Licensed Professional Counselor with advanced certifications in integrated marriage and family therapy, death and grief therapy, substance abuse and addiction therapy, crisis and abuse therapy, temperament therapy, child and adolescent therapy, group therapy, domestic violence and intervention therapy, sexual therapy, and cognitive therapy. She is a board-certified master mental health professional, board-certified master life coach, certified international motivational speaker, and multi-award winner; including the Governor's Citation from Wes Moore, Maryland's first Black Governor, Indy Author Legacy Award, My Sister Keeper's Phenomenal Woman Award, and the Speak Life Award. She is an 11X bestselling author and 6X international bestselling author. Her inaugural solo project *"Don't Quit: Motivation To Reach Your Goals"* sold in Antigua, Canada, and the UK and continues to motivate and inspire families around the world.

Furthermore, she serves as a mental health professional, so blessed and grateful to have served as a Moderator (in conjunction with Dr. Jennifer Jones Bryant) of the Professional Mental Health Series, a community giveback program provided through her 501 (c)(3) organization, which addresses the global mental health crisis. The series provides a professional platform to help remove mental health stigmas one mind at a time. Her organization also provides pro bono, professional counseling and mental health coaching, mentoring and support for doctoral candidates, emergency funding for seniors, holiday meals, scholarships for summer camp, and so much more to the community. Lastly, she has served as an international representative for twelve years, and ten years as a clinical supervisor for a counseling organization.

Affectionately known as the "Master Motivational Mindset Coach," Dr. Huntley motivates, captivates, and elevates others through her high-octane motivations® . She has been featured in *Brainz Magazine, VIP Global Magazine, Faith Heart International Magazine, Glambitious Magazine, Voyage Atl, Bold Journey Magazine, UP WORD Global Magazine, I Am Bold And Fearless Woman Magazine,* and Making Headline News. She has been featured on Radio One, and Impact the World Radio (VOXWAV). Her narrative and unwavering mustard seed faith in God will unequivocally motivate you to rise up, speak up, and follow up!

You may connect with her via the following:

Website: www.drmaryjhuntley.com
Facebook: Dr. Mary J Huntley
Instagram: authordrmaryjhuntley
LinkedIn: Dr. Mary J. Huntley

FOREWORD

"For I know the plans I have for you, declares the Lord, plans to prosper you and not to harm you, plans to give you hope and a future." Jeremiah 29:11

Dr. Mary J. Huntley is a wordsmith, and renowned author who has written several Amazon #1 international bestsellers, and her work has left a lasting impact on the literary landscape, captivating the hearts and minds of countless readers. With gratitude and honor, I accepted her invitation to write the Foreword and serve as the Executive Strategic Advisor for the *Trust the Process: Reap the Harvest Anthology*. Because of her commitment to integrity, truth, and self-investment, two years ago, I extended an invitation to her to act in the same capacity for my book, *Step Into Leadership Greatness, Volumes 1 and 2*, which became international bestsellers.

Our authentic partnership is one that's built on trust, open communication, and mutual respect. We offer encouragement to one another and share what's on our hearts often to overcome challenges, develop creative solutions, and motivate each other to be our best selves. Collaborating has also helped us to improve our skills and achieve great results. While trusting the process we have reaped the rewards of our hard work. Our teamwork has created a synergy that has enhanced the outcomes of our successful projects and fostered personal growth.

I have had an all-access pass that has allowed me to sit in her front row, navigate behind the scenes, and work alongside her for many years. I have had the privilege of cheering her on, applauding, and celebrating her as she earned various awards and secured her seat at phenomenal entrepreneurial tables. Last year was exceptional for Dr. Huntley as she was awarded a Citation for her leadership and community service work from Wes Moore, Maryland's first Black Governor, and she received the United States Presidential

Lifetime Achievement Award. She also is the recent recipient of My Sister Keeper's Phenomenal Woman Award.

Dr. Huntley and I enjoy our collaborative partnership. She is the Chief Executive/Encouragement Officer of Trinity Global Empowerment Ministries, Inc., while I am the Executive Founder of Reaching Within, An Empowerment Journey LLC. We are passionate about empowering others. She was a major supporter, strategic partner, and sponsor of my initial "Step Into Leadership Greatness Summit." She gave back to the community by providing several scholarships for individuals to receive board-certified professional mental health coaching certifications. We're advocates for mental health, hosting weekly panel discussions designed to remove the stigma that's often attached to the various conditions, as well as equipping our audiences with knowledge and resources that are applicable and beneficial to their healing. Dr. Huntley has exceptional project management skills and when she started laying the groundwork for this anthology, she used them to guide and motivate the authors each step of the way. She kept an open mind as we navigated the publishing process, knowing that in the end, a magnificent masterpiece would be born.

Allow me to share with you my personal story of trusting the process. Ten years ago, a woman named Dr. Celeste Owens introduced me to a 40-day surrender fast, and I decided to try it again in 2015. I prayed and pondered about the one thing in my life I wanted to surrender. I needed much relief from the black cloud that was hanging over my head — an unaffordable mortgage! It was the one thing that kept me up at night so much so that I decided to relinquish control of trying to fix the loan.

I purchased my first home in 2001, and by 2015 my monthly payment for my current home had more than doubled to nearly $3,900 because of ill-advised refinancing decisions. Additionally, I had $100K of negative amortization because the mortgage loan payment was less than the interest, coupled with lagging home prices. I never missed a mortgage payment. However, I was denied relief for almost five years, though I'd contacted several sources, and responded to their requests. I felt hopeless and trapped, and experienced many sleepless nights. I was ready to walk away with my family and allow the mortgage company to do a short sale. However, my miracle occurred during the last week of the 40-day surrender fast. I knew that it would take a miracle, and God showed up and showed off. My loan was fixed through a settlement agreement after one of the loan representatives used my credit information for his gain. My monthly mortgage payment was reduced by more than $1,000 and nearly $100K interest was removed. What I learned from this experience, with tears of joy streaming down my face is that "impossible" always succumbs to God's matchless power.

There are other compelling, miraculous stories that showcase individuals pursuing their dreams, undergoing transformative exploration while embracing uncertainty, and growing through each step of the journey. The experiences and lessons shared by these authors serve as guiding lights, reminding us of the grit and determination required to overcome obstacles and dominate our uniquely created paths. On the pages that follow, you will encounter insights, strategies, and practical tools to help you embrace the process and channel it toward your goals. From techniques that cultivate patience and perseverance to methods for reframing failures and rejections as opportunities for growth, this book will empower and inspire you.

Moreover, this anthology will encourage us to find joy and fulfillment in the journey rather than solely focusing on the destination. It will challenge us to appreciate the small victories and find meaning in every step forward, savoring the lessons and experiences that shape us. Trusting the process can be challenging, and there will be doubt, uncertainty, and frustration. However, know that you are not alone on this journey. Let us embark on this transformative path together, supporting and celebrating each other, as well as our collective growth. The harvest that awaits at the end of the process is often more rewarding than we could ever imagine. One author shared, **"God uses and recycles our most painful experiences for a better purpose."**

Another author stated, **"In life, the journey is as important as the destination."** As gentle whispers in our ears, these phenomenal authors remind us that great things come to those who trust the process, cultivate patience, and dare to take bold steps toward their dreams, all while embracing the growth and abundance that comes with the process through the following five ways:

Embracing Uncertainty:

1.   **"I felt the peace of this future dated me and embraced the feeling fully. This shift defused my feelings of trepidation and significantly calmed my doubt."** A key aspect of trusting the process is embracing uncertainty. Life is full of unexpected twists and turns, and predicting every outcome is impossible. Instead of fearing the unknown, learn to embrace it. When we accept that we cannot control everything, it opens us up to new possibilities and opportunities, allowing us to let go of the need for immediate results and focus on future rewards.

Learning from Setbacks:

2.   **"Life will be a mixture of wins and failures. This part is true, but when you trust the process, the reward will always be wonderful because you will either learn a lesson or receive a blessing."** Trusting the process also means instead of viewing setbacks as roadblocks, we see them as opportunities for growth. Each failure provides valuable lessons and insights, helping us refine our approach and make better decisions in the future.

Building Resilience and Fulfillment:

3.   **"Rejection serves as a redirection; a closed door can create opportunities for new doors to open that we would not have discovered if it wasn't for the "no" we received."** Resilience is the ability to adapt and recover from adversity, a crucial trait for success. Rather than becoming discouraged by adversity, resilience allows us to bounce back and keep moving forward. **"Through the twists and turns, the setbacks and victories, I discovered the true essence of trusting the process – a journey that led to the fulfillment of a promise and the realization of a dream."**

Staying Focused on the Journey:

4.   **"Doubt, skepticism, and disillusionment can threaten to undermine one's faith and erode the foundations of trust that have been cultivated."** Trusting the process reminds us that while goals are important, it's equally important to enjoy the process of working toward them. We can find joy and fulfillment in the small victories by staying present and engaged in the journey, allowing us to appreciate our growth and progress regardless of the outcome.

Cultivating Faith and Patience:

5.   Patience is a virtue when it comes to trusting the process. **"Almost everything you want to do in life has a process you must complete."** It's natural to want immediate results, but true growth and success take time. By cultivating patience, we can avoid becoming discouraged or giving up prematurely. Progress may be slow, but success often requires persistence and perseverance.

In conclusion, trusting the process in order to reap the harvest is not always easy, but it is a mindset that can lead to personal growth, resilience, and success. **"Keeping the faith while treading lightly through storms allows us to find our footing**

again." As you embark on this journey of trusting the process, I encourage you to embrace curiosity, open-mindedness, and a commitment to personal growth. Reflect on your experiences and consider how cultivating trust can bring about profound transformations in your life. By embracing uncertainty, learning from setbacks, building resilience, staying focused on the journey, and cultivating patience, we can navigate life's challenges with confidence and optimism, letting go of the need for immediate results and instead focusing on the present moment and its lessons.

Believe in the process, ignite your faith, demonstrate resilience, and cherish the journey toward your bountiful harvest!

Dr. Jennifer Jones Bryant is passionate about helping mid-level career women discover and cultivate their inner strength, enabling them to reach the next level in their careers. Her core message revolves around the importance of reaching within oneself, making a positive impact, and staying true to one's values and beliefs. She is a Fortune 100 senior leader of Associate Experience (Chief of Staff), where she oversees the continuous improvement of associate engagement, culture, diversity, inclusion, and belonging, as well as overall organizational effectiveness. She focuses on four key areas: enablement, inclusion, engagement, and leadership. She also leads one of the largest women's empowerment business resource groups with more than 20,000 members. Before joining the Fortune 100 company, she spent 31 years working for the federal government. Her career spanned various functional areas, from clerk-typist to Executive Director, where she led teams in business management services, process improvements, and employee engagement. Her exceptional performance has been recognized through numerous awards, including the United States Presidential Lifetime Achievement Award for leadership, customer service, innovation, civil rights, diversity, and inclusion initiatives. As an accomplished author and speaker with decades of leadership experience, she is in high demand, regularly receiving invitations to speak at federal agencies, academia, and community organizations. She has been featured in prominent publications such as *Essence Magazine*, *Brainz Magazine*, and *VIP Global*

Magazine. Additionally, she has been interviewed by various media outlets, including Radio One, WTOP, and WUSA's Great Day Washington.

ECCLESIASTES 3

A Time for Everything

[1] For everything there is a season,
   a time for every activity under heaven.
[2] A time to be born and a time to die.
   A time to plant and a time to harvest.
[3] A time to kill and a time to heal.
   A time to tear down and a time to build up.
[4] A time to cry and a time to laugh.
   A time to grieve and a time to dance.
[5] A time to scatter stones and a time to gather stones.
   A time to embrace and a time to turn away.
[6] A time to search and a time to quit searching.
   A time to keep and a time to throw away.
[7] A time to tear and a time to mend.
   A time to be quiet and a time to speak.
[8] A time to love and a time to hate.
   A time for war and a time for peace.

[9] What do people really get for all their hard work? [10] I have seen the burden God has placed on us all. [11] Yet God has made everything beautiful for its own time. He has planted eternity in the human heart, but even so, people cannot see the whole scope of God's work from beginning to end. [12] So I concluded there is nothing better than to be happy and enjoy ourselves as long as we can. [13] And people should eat and drink and enjoy the fruits of their labor, for these are gifts from God.

[14] And I know that whatever God does is final. Nothing can be added to it or taken from it. God's purpose is that people should fear him. [15] What is happening now has happened before, and what will happen in the future has happened before, because God makes the same things happen over and over again.

The Injustices of Life

[16] I also noticed that under the sun there is evil in the courtroom. Yes, even the courts of law are corrupt! [17] I said to myself, "In due season God will judge everyone, both good and bad, for all their deeds."

[18] I also thought about the human condition—how God proves to people that they are like animals. [19] For people and animals share the same fate—both breathe[a] and both must die. So people have no real advantage over the animals. How meaningless! [20] Both go to the same place—they came from dust, and they return to dust. [21] For who can prove that the human spirit goes up and the spirit of animals goes down into the earth? [22] So I saw that there is nothing better for people than to be happy in their work. That is our lot in life. And no one can bring us back to see what happens after we die.

PURPOSE: "Until purpose is discovered existence has no meaning." - Dr. Myles Munroe.

There are no words to describe the sense of satisfaction or fulfillment you feel when you are living in your purpose daily. That should be our desire and goal on a regular basis. It is indescribable when you realize that you were born to fulfill a specific assignment. And until you discover that assignment, you will not be your best self. Individuals walk away from high-profile, well-paying jobs because they are not fulfilled. **Life simply has no meaning for them because they have not discovered their purpose and they are not being fulfilled.** According to Dr. Myles Munroe, *"Purpose is the original intent in the mind of the creator that motivated him to create a particular item. It is the why that explains the reason for existence. "Every product is the child of purpose. Until purpose is discovered, existence has no meaning."*

Dr. Abraham Maslow substantiates our need for fulfillment in the chart below.

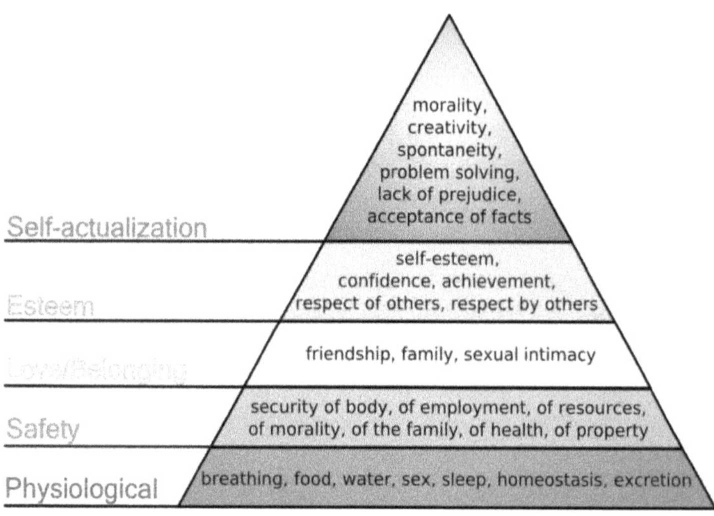

At the very peak of Maslow's hierarchy are the self-actualization needs, referring to what people must achieve in order to reach their full potential. *"What a man can be, he must be,"* Maslow explained.

Overwhelmed to Overcomer: Trusting the Process for a Divine Harvest

DR. RHONDA WOOD

In the journey of life, we often encounter seasons of waiting and uncertainty. During these times, our faith is tested, and we may find ourselves questioning the purpose behind the challenges we face. As Christians, the concept of trusting the process and reaping the harvest is deeply rooted in our understanding of God's character, His divine timing, and His perfect plan for our lives.

I remember a time in June 2015 when I was approached by a recruiter about a high-level position at a new company. I had hit a glass ceiling at my current company, so this sounded like the perfect opportunity – a prestigious company, challenging role, excellent benefits package, and bigger salary. It was undoubtedly a dream job, but I remember praying, "God, if this is not from you, I don't want it." I prayed during every phase of the process – the application, several rounds of interviews, and the submission of writing samples. When I received the official offer of employment, I was ready to resign from my current position and move on to something greater.

The first few months of my position were great. The lawyers seemed excited to have me on board, and my supervisor appeared to appreciate my hard work. But within a year, things quickly changed. My supervisor grew cold. My colleagues became bullies. The workload was unbearable. In an attempt to stay ahead and keep up, I often arrived at work early, worked through lunch, stayed late, logged on from home at the end of the business day, and was on call via a mobile device on some weekends. I was overworked and overwhelmed. To make matters worse, my long working hours were beginning to affect me personally and professionally.

Like every mother, I dreamed of a life full of love, laughter, and a bright future for my child. But those dreams changed dramatically when my daughter began to have difficulties with her mental health at home and school. As a single mom, my road was already challenging. I was trying to do a great job at work as a new manager and at home as a mother, but I felt the heaviness of the weight of my situation on my shoulders.

I remember falling to my knees in my office. I put my face on the floor with tears running down my face. I remember crying out to God and questioning why he allowed all this to happen. I remember praying to him about the job that now felt too difficult to handle. Through tears, I asked God, "Why did you bring me here just to fail?" I felt embarrassed, humiliated, and ashamed. I didn't want my employer to think they had made a mistake hiring me and that I couldn't handle the job and responsibilities. I was shunned at work, abandoned by family, and looked down on at church.

Filled with uncertainty about how I would support my family and after much prayer, I decided to take a leave of absence from work to prioritize our mental health through talk therapy, support groups, and other resources. I could have let this difficult moment dictate my future, but my story is a reminder that God can turn the deepest pain into His perfection.

A few months after taking leave from my job, I was contacted by the National Alliance on Mental Illness of Prince George's County, who invited me to speak on a panel. They wanted me to share my story of supporting a loved one with a mental health condition. I had never shared my story publicly. Nonetheless, I agreed. After sharing my story and walking off the stage, I was amazed at how many people came up to me to share how my story impacted their lives. There was a single mother at her wit's end, a career woman ready to resign, and a police officer wanting more education on mental health in the community. And an elected official wanted me to speak to his youth group. I felt so inspired that I knew I had discovered my passion and purpose.

Speaking and sharing my story has made me feel so internally fulfilled because I get to help transform lives. I began to aggressively pursue speaking and coaching as a business, and I started to receive opportunities to share my message of empowerment around the world on stages, television, talk shows, radio, podcasts, magazines, and on the news. Everything happens for a reason. If I had never been made uncomfortable, especially during a challenging time, I never would have been open to embarking on something new. And I would not be where I am today – living in my passion and purpose with no regrets. Remarkably, my daughter followed in my footsteps and now advocates, speaks, and writes about the mental health stigma among teens and young adults.

God uses and recycles our most painful experiences for a better purpose. Perhaps you, like me, find yourself wandering the detours of life. Don't allow your painful moments to hold you hostage and keep you from propelling into your future. Regardless of how lost you feel, you, too, can reap the harvest of God's blessings and leave an impact on this world.

During a difficult time in my life, I felt completely crushed by stress and worry. I remember crying out to God, telling Him I hated what I was going through but loved Him. I believed that whatever I was experiencing was for my own good and would help me become a better person. I trusted in the idea that God had already started a good work in me and that He would bring it to completion.

Throughout the Bible, God provides us with promises affirming His faithfulness and assures us that our trust in Him will be rewarded. I simply had to trust the process (his plan, promises, and perfect timing) to reap the harvest, by executing my helpful tips below:

1.   **Trusting His Plan**: Proverbs 3:5-6 (NIV) reminds us, "Trust in the Lord with all your heart and lean not on your own understanding; in all your ways submit to him, and he will make your paths straight." Trusting the process involves surrendering our desires and plans to God and acknowledging His sovereignty over our lives. It requires patience, faith, and an unwavering belief that God works behind the scenes for our good. In Isaiah 55:8-9 (NIV), God declares, "For my thoughts are not your thoughts, neither are your ways my ways, declares the Lord. As the heavens are higher than the earth, so are my ways higher than your ways and my thoughts than your thoughts." Even when we can't comprehend the intricacies of God's plan, we must trust that His ways are higher, and His timing is perfect.

2.   **Trusting His Promises**: Ecclesiastes 3:1 (NIV) reminds us, "There is a time for everything and a season for every activity under the heavens." Just as there is a season for planting, there is also a season for harvesting. Trusting the process involves recognizing that God's timing is crucial for manifesting His promises. James 5:7 (NIV) encourages us with these words, "Be patient, then, brothers and sisters, until the Lord's coming. See how the farmer waits for the land to yield its valuable crop, patiently waiting for the autumn and spring rains." The farmer's patience in waiting for the right seasons reflects the patience we must cultivate as we await the fulfillment of God's promises.

3.   **Trusting His Perfect Timing:** Galatians 6:9 (NIV): "Let us not become weary in doing good, for at the proper time we will reap a harvest if we do not give up." This verse encourages us to persevere in our faith and good works, knowing that a bountiful

harvest awaits us in God's perfect timing. Psalm 37:4 (NIV): "Take delight in the Lord, and he will give you the desires of your heart." Trusting the process involves finding joy in our relationship with God, knowing that as we align our desires with His will, He will grant them at the appointed time. Trusting the process and reaping the harvest are important parts of the Christian journey. As we go through times of waiting and uncertainty, we should hold onto God's promises and have confidence that His plan for our lives is perfect. By having faith, patience, and an unshakeable trust in God's sovereignty, we can look forward to the abundant harvest that awaits us in His perfect timing.

Dr. Rhonda M. Wood is an award-winning international keynoter, bestselling author, media personality, and a leading authority on mental health. Once a corporate professional projecting an image of having it all together externally, she silently grappled with daily challenges of depression, anxiety, and lingering repercussions from unresolved childhood trauma. After finally seeking out therapy, she now shares her mental health journey with a level of transparency that resonates with women worldwide, inspired by her bold approach to life and healing. Her unique voice and talents allow her to serve women from all walks of life, from the classroom to the boardroom.

REFLECTION PAGE

How did the author's story resonate with you? How did the story encourage you? Do you feel that you can execute the tips shared while trusting the process to reap an overwhelmingly successful harvest? Explain below.

REFLECTION PAGE

Soaring Above The Clouds

DENNIKA DAVENPORT

One of my favorite modes of travel is by plane, though it hasn't always been. At one time, the thought of traveling to a new destination via a metal tube suspended thousands of miles in the air engendered fear, angst, and suffocating dread. Thankfully, I overcame the fear and now look forward to this magnificent form of travel that humans have indulged in for hundreds of years. Traveling by plane serves as a metaphor for our lives. The power of releasing ourselves to the much anticipated take off, exhilarating G-force of ascending to unknown heights, and even navigating rocky and unsettling turbulence, gives us a blueprint for facing life's challenges. Success depends on learning to trust the process on the road to our destinations and will ultimately yield a bountiful harvest far beyond our wildest dreams.

While traveling on a business trip for my dream job a few months ago, I found myself sitting on the tarmac for what seemed like hours, waiting for the plane to take off without much communication from the flight crew. My mind drifted while crunched between two obviously frustrated and concerned strangers. I thought of how this predicament would have evoked uncontrollable sweating, choking panic, and an irrepressible need to exit the plane just a few months earlier. Simultaneously, I was reminded of the rocky road to finding my dream job and how it mimicked this situation.

My four-month job search included more than 300 applications and 10 interviews. It yielded extreme frustration, self-doubt, and similar to turbulent plane travel, a need to exit the predicament quickly. The paths to overcoming both hurdles were parallel. Both called for trusting the process on the road to my destiny.

While boarding the flight and returning from my first business trip, I assumed the flight would last no more than three short hours, as predicted. The weather was fair, and there was no indication of plane issues or malfunctions. I learned quickly; that my assumption was incorrect. Similarly, when I started my search for a new job after an abrupt, yet necessary departure from another employer, I anticipated the search would only last a few short weeks. I was convinced that two advanced degrees and more than 30 years of diverse experience in one industry would quickly open a multitude of lucrative employment doors. This assumption was far from reality. I needed to craft a plan to navigate both challenges to soar above the threatening clouds coming my way.

Trust The Pilot

After waiting about an hour on the tarmac, I began to ask the question, "When?" I wondered when we would finally take off and when I would arrive home and see my family again. Finally, the captain's deep but comforting voice came over the intercom and explained why we were not moving. He shared that the plane was having mechanical issues, assured us that everything would be fine, and offered us the option of exiting the plane or staying aboard while it was repaired. I realized I had a decision to make. I could allow fear to consume me or focus on the pilot's comforting words. I decided to trust the pilot instead of embracing the paralyzing fear determined to control my thoughts. I promptly exited the plane while mechanical repairs were made. Trusting the pilot meant releasing the outcome and trusting in what I couldn't see.

In the same vein, after about a month of job searching, my energy remained high, but doubt began to creep in. Each morning, my first sip of coffee from my favorite mug was accompanied by a looming question, "When?" I asked myself when this search would end and when an employer would see my worth and ask me to join their organization. While glancing out of my office window one afternoon, I realized I needed to decide how to handle the fears and increasing doubt I was experiencing. I chose to trust the pilot of the process. For me, this meant trusting God and resting in the unseen future.

See Yourself In The Future

A few hours of waiting in the airport yielded a bit of panic and restlessness. I wondered if we were ever going to start our trip. I even pondered renting a van and driving home. In my panic-ravaged brain, a 19-hour drive at night was a viable alternative to waiting countless hours to take off and begin the journey home. The lightbulb moment came when I recalled one of my favorite songs by Bishop Paul S. Morton. In his song, "Be Blessed," he sings, "I see you in your future..." As I continued waiting, I visualized myself on the plane and arriving home safely. The peace of this future dated me and embraced the feeling fully. This shift defused my feelings of trepidation and significantly calmed my doubt and anxiousness.

The third month of my job search took an emotional toll just as waiting at the airport did. After a few interviews with no job offer, I asked myself if I was truly qualified for the jobs for which I was applying. I felt desperate and started applying for any job I could find. Many roles were far below my skill set and compensation requirement, but I was consumed by self-doubt and thoughts of the due dates of my growing list of bills. During a brief conversation with my fiancé, he mentioned, "You should only apply for positions that represent your future." This statement revolutionized my thinking and caused me to veer in a completely different direction. Immediately, I began visualizing myself in my dream job while searching for new opportunities. Armed with this revelation, I commenced only looking for positions worthy of my experience and education. This shift helped me cast a much smaller job search net and focused my energy on the direction of my vision.

Find The Joy

As the hands on the clock continued to progress, there was no sign we would be leaving the airport. To calm my worrisome thoughts, I started walking around and noticing the passengers. I wondered about their stories, where they were going, and how their lives differed from my own. I admired the beauty of the airport architecture and how far I'd come on my travel journey. I even started a conversation with a fellow passenger and learned she was a neighbor. Allowing myself to feel joy and open to other thoughts created an enjoyable experience despite the delays and angst of the journey.

Similarly, as my job search crept toward four months, I changed my thinking and sought reasons for gratitude when I felt fear and doubt blanketing my exhausted mind. Trusting the process meant remaining thankful and grateful for my past and present. I chose to focus on my many blessings, including a healthy body, a wonderful partner, a beautiful home, reliable transportation, and a supportive family. That paradigm shift was invaluable in my journey and transformed the atmosphere of my experience.

As I changed my thinking in both situations, I found myself preparing to soar above the clouds of my fear, worry, and frustration. Once I shifted my thoughts to the airport, we were redirected to another plane and quickly headed to our destination. Remarkably, as I redirected my thoughts during the job search, I received two amazing job offers, accepted the one that was my dream come true, and negotiated the highest salary of my long career.

To soar above the inevitable clouds of our lives, we must envision our destination, decide on a path to get there, and prepare for and accept the highs and lows of the journey to unimagined altitudes. All of this amounts to trusting the process of our lives. Trusting the process is challenging at times, but the following recipe yielded a harvest far beyond my wildest dreams and imagination:

1.   **Trust The Pilot** • The pilot ultimately determines the trajectory of your journey. Faith in your pilot will allow you to navigate the bumps and unavoidable turbulence accompanying every expedition. Surrendering to your pilot and knowing the chosen path will lead to your harvest.

2.   **See Yourself In The Future** • Every journey's starting point looks markedly different from the destination. Seeing yourself in your future doesn't deny your current circumstances, but it gives you the altitude to climb above any dark and ominous clouds to see the future and ultimately reach your goals. Creating a vision board is a great way to embrace the future you.

3.   **Find The Joy** • Often, joy is hidden amid the tiny details of our challenges. Seeking and focusing on our blessings in each moment serves as a buffer against the rough air currents that often blow our way. Creating a brag book of your previous successes and keeping a list of blessings to refer to in tough times is a great way to start embracing your joy.

Dennika Davenport has more than 30 years of HR management experience in healthcare, oil and gas, engineering, and law. She currently serves as the Director of Human Resources for one of the world's largest engineering firms, where she oversees HR initiatives for more than 30 offices in the United States. She holds a B.S. degree in Psychology and an MBA from the University of Maryland's Global Campus and is currently seeking an M.S. in Clinical Mental Health Counseling from Walden University. Also to her credit, she holds an SHRM-SCP designation. She is the owner of HERRS, a life coaching business helping black and brown women reinvent their lives.

You can learn more about her via www.herr's.live, or LinkedIn https://www.linkedin.com/in/dennikadavenport.

REFLECTION PAGE

How did the author's story resonate with you? How did the story encourage you? Do you feel that you can execute the tips shared while trusting the process to reap an overwhelmingly successful harvest? Explain below.

REFLECTION PAGE

A Journey That Led to Fulfillment

Nadia Monsano

In the quaint town of Germantown, Maryland, I embarked on a journey that would teach me the true meaning of trusting the process. With dreams of becoming a successful public relations representative, I started My Sister Keeper, a boutique PR agency that aimed to help businesses shine in the public eye. Little did I know that the path to success would be fraught with unexpected twists and turns.

My journey began with a passion for connecting businesses with their audience. Armed with a solid business plan and unwavering determination, I set out to make My Sister Keeper a beacon of trust and reliability in the world of public relations. The early days were challenging, but I held onto the belief that success would come with hard work and perseverance.

As the months passed, my organization started gaining recognition in the local business community. I secured a few notable clients, and my reputation as a PR expert grew. I was living my dream, basking in the joy of helping businesses build their brands and establish a positive public image.

However, the unforeseen challenges of 2020 were about to reshape the course of my entrepreneurial journey. The global pandemic hit, casting a shadow of uncertainty over businesses worldwide. With events canceled, storefronts closed, and the economy in turmoil, the world of public relations was facing unprecedented challenges. Suddenly, the clients I had worked so hard to acquire were no longer interested in public relations services. I was left with a business that was no longer sustainable.

I could have given up, but I knew that wasn't an option. In those dark times, I found solace in my faith. Turning to the Bible for guidance, I stumbled upon Proverbs 3:5-6, "Trust in the Lord with all your heart and lean not on your own understanding; in all your ways submit to him, and he will make your paths straight." This verse became my anchor, a reminder to trust the process even when it seemed unclear.

With a heavy heart, I realized that the traditional PR approach might not be sustainable in the face of the pandemic. It was time to pivot and rewrite the business plan that had once guided me to success. Instead of succumbing to despair, I chose to embrace the uncertainty and look for new opportunities.

I also drew inspiration from Isaiah 43:19, "Behold, I am doing a new thing; now it springs forth, do you not perceive it? I will make a way in the wilderness and rivers in the desert." I set out on a new path. My skills as a graphic designer, a hobby I had cultivated over the years, became the key to unlocking a fresh chapter for My Sister Keeper.

It wasn't long before I realized that my passion for design could be the key to my success. I had always enjoyed creating graphics and layouts, but I had never considered it as a career path. However, with the pandemic forcing businesses to shift to online platforms, I saw an opportunity to help them present themselves professionally through their online branding.

Reinventing myself as a graphic designer meant investing in my own growth and development. I dedicated countless hours to honing my craft, poring over design tutorials, attending workshops, and experimenting with different styles and techniques. It was a humbling experience, realizing that mastery in one field did not guarantee success in another. Yet, with each new skill acquired and each project completed, my confidence grew.

One of the biggest challenges was building a client base from scratch. In the world of public relations, networking, and word-of-mouth referrals had been the lifeblood of my business. Now, as a graphic designer, I had to start from square one, reaching out to potential clients and showcasing my portfolio in hopes of securing projects.

There were moments of doubt and frustration along the way. I questioned whether I had made the right decision to pivot my business and whether I had what it took to succeed in this new venture. Yet, in those moments of uncertainty, I leaned on my faith, trusting that God had a plan for me and that every challenge was an opportunity for growth.

Proverbs 16:3 became my guiding light, "Commit to the Lord whatever you do, and he will establish your plans." With each setback, I reminded myself to surrender control and trust in God's timing. I poured my heart and soul into every design project, knowing that my efforts were not in vain.

Slowly but surely, my perseverance began to pay off. Through word-of-mouth referrals and networking within the design community, I started landing my first clients. Each project served as a stepping stone, building my reputation as a reliable and talented graphic designer.

With determination and creativity, I transformed my boutique PR agency into an international graphic design studio. The pivot was not without its challenges, but I held onto the promise in Romans 8:28, "And we know that in all things God works for the good of those who love him, who have been called according to his purpose."

The global shift to virtual platforms created a demand for a visually appealing and professional online presence. My Sister Keeper became a beacon of hope for businesses struggling to adapt. Through innovative graphic design, we helped businesses showcase their products and services in a digital landscape.

The journey from PR representative to international graphic designer taught me the importance of adaptability and resilience. When the road seemed uncertain, I learned to trust the process and lean on my faith. Philippians 4:6-7 became my mantra, "Do not be anxious about anything, but in every situation, by prayer and petition, with thanksgiving, present your requests to God. And the peace of God, which transcends all understanding, will guard your hearts and your minds in Christ Jesus."

The success of My Sister Keeper in the realm of international graphic design was a testament to the power of faith and perseverance. I found fulfillment in helping businesses not only survive but thrive in the digital age. My Sister Keeper's portfolio expanded to include clients from diverse industries and corners of the globe.

In 2023, My Sister Keeper hosted an event that celebrated 40 phenomenal women from different walks of life. The event was called the Phenomenal Woman Awards, and it was a night to remember. The honorees were selected based on their exceptional contributions to their communities and their impact on the lives of others. The event was attended by family, friends, and supporters. One of the highlights of the evening was the announcement that because of the partnership between My Sister Keeper and 10 other organizations in the United States and throughout the world, they were able to receive donations. This was a testament to the commitment of My Sister Keeper to give back to the community. The Phenomenal Woman Awards is now an anticipated event every year and because of its success, it will now be held annually. My Sister Keeper is committed to recognizing and celebrating the achievements of women.

I have now started the *My Sister Keeper Magazine* line. I feature women from all walks of life both in the United States and internationally. I am blessed to meet amazing women who are making an impact on the lives of so many individuals. Using my graphic design skills to not only create professional designs for clients but to make an impact in the community through my magazine, apparel line, and podcast gives me great pleasure.

The story comes full circle as My Sister Keeper, now a flourishing international graphic design studio, collaborates with business owners locally and internationally. Our mission is to empower businesses to show up online in a professional manner, leaving a lasting impression on their target audience. Through the twists and turns, the setbacks and victories, I discovered the true essence of trusting the process – a journey that led to the fulfillment of a promise and the realization of a dream. I am not sure what stage you are in while navigating your process. However, I would like to share a few tips below that may help you to stay the course:

1.   Understand that delay does not mean denial. I knew within my heart of hearts that I possessed the characteristics to become an awesome graphic designer. However, I kept hitting a brick wall. Sometimes you will not reach your destination until all things are properly aligned and you are ready for your audience, and your audience is ready for you.

2.   Trust God even when you can't trace Him. Sometimes your path may be filled with unconventional twists and turns. Be not dismayed as long as you know that YOUR Pilot is well able to deliver you to your assigned destination.

3.   Persevere and allow patience to have her perfect work. Character is cultivated and built during our most challenging moments. "But let patience have her perfect work, that ye may be perfect and entire, wanting nothing."

Nadia Monsano is an accomplished 6x international bestselling author and a marketing and branding specialist. She served our country for 10 years in the United States Army and retired as a staff sergeant. During her time in the military, she served one tour in Iraq and earned the prestigious Iraqi Freedom Medal of Honor. She is the proud recipient of the Presidential Lifetime Achievement Award and the Woman of Heart Award. An internationally recognized speaker, Nadia shares her expertise on the importance of having a positive mindset. She is also the co-chair of The Women's Round Table Action Platform of Trinidad and Tobago.

REFLECTION PAGE

How did the author's story resonate with you? How did the story encourage you? Do you feel that you can execute the tips shared while trusting the process to reap an overwhelmingly successful harvest? Explain below.

REFLECTION PAGE

The Five-Step Process to Success and Fulfillment

DR. THERESA MOSELEY

Almost everything you want to do in life involves a process. If you want to join the military, there is a process. When you select a college, in order to be accepted, there's a process to follow. When you get married, there is a process until the day of the event. One thing in life that everyone must develop and then follow is the process. I believe everyone is born with a gift and a divine assignment. The process of developing that gift includes being nurtured as a child and continuing through adulthood. When parents, teachers, family, and friends recognize the special gifts that we all possess, it is easier to determine life's purpose. I believe when people live their purpose, they will be successful, fulfilled, prosperous, and have inner peace. There is a process to know, implement, and accept your divine assignment.

First, you need to know who you are. Self-awareness is very important. You must be able to understand your emotions and thoughts and recognize your strengths and weaknesses. Not only will self-awareness help you in the work world, but it will also help in developing strong relationships. You must also discover your passion. Do what you love!

Think about what you loved to do as a child. For me, it was playing with my Barbie dolls. I had 40 of them and would line them up as if they were on an airplane, and I was the flight attendant who made all the announcements. I even had luggage for some of the dolls. Twenty years later, I was employed by an airline. I love to travel and sometimes feel like I live on a plane. Other times when playing with my dolls, I would arrange them in four rows of 10, classroom style. I was an educator for 28 years. I loved working with students and teachers and eventually became a high school principal. I realized that my passion was working with people; however, I was a little confused about my purpose until I read Jeremiah 29:11: "For I know the plans I have for you, declared the LORD. Plans to prosper you and not harm you. Plans to give you hope and a future."

I prayed to God for the wisdom to determine what I needed to do to make a difference in the world. I woke up one morning and realized all the trials and tribulations I went through in life were preparing me for my divine assignment to make the world a more peaceful place. With all the lessons learned; I can share them with the world. One day while I was journaling and writing reflections, I decided to start writing positive self-reflection affirmations. I posted them on mirrors and wrote them in my journal. As a child, I was very small and skinny. I was always the last chosen because people perceived me as weak. To combat that negative childhood trauma, I wrote: I am strong and resilient. I am confident. I am worthy. I deserve love and happiness. I also wrote short and long-term goals, both professionally and personally. I monitored my goals every Sunday and adjusted as needed. I joined several groups and networked with people of like minds.

My life changed when I lost two students to violence. It was an awakening. I knew I had to do more. My heart was broken and the violence in the world was worsening. President Barack Obama once said, "Every life must be given a chance to reach its full potential. Every life matters." My two students had dreams and goals that would never be fulfilled. I felt like I was successful in my professional career, but I was not fulfilled. I went to a master class where the instructor quoted Mark Twain, "There are two days that are important. The day you were born and the day you find out why." On that day, I recognized that my gift was my voice. My passion was serving others, and my purpose was making the world a more peaceful place. I decided to start a business and provide services to schools and corporate America on how to have a peaceful climate. I started speaking and writing books on inner and world peace. I had the pleasure of meeting Claes Nobel in 2007. My daughter was a Nobel Scholar. During the National Society of High School Scholars ceremony in Atlanta, Claes said, "You all have proved you are academic scholars. Now go into the world and become ambassadors of peace." This statement resonated with me; therefore, I named my company TAM Creating Ambassadors of Peace LLC.

Once I started my business, training organizations, and speaking around the world, I realized that I could teach people how to live out their purpose through a five-step process. It's the same process I used that led me to create generational wealth and leave a legacy for my family. The five-step process is as follows:

1.   Self-Awareness.
2.   Know your passion.
3.   Develop a blueprint.
4.   Monitor/Accountability.
5.   Networking.

The first step is **self-awareness**. It's important to know who you are and to always be your authentic self. Often people behave based on how others think they should. They listen to negative talk, pretend to like things they don't like, and sometimes laugh at things that are not funny. They conform to what others think they should be. These people often develop imposter syndrome. Two ways to combat this are through positive self-talk and surrounding yourself with positive people.

The second step is **knowing your passion.** Bishop T.D. Jakes said, "If you don't know your purpose, follow your passion. Your passion will lead you to your purpose." There is a Japanese philosophy called "Ikigai" which means "a reason for being" and is designed to help you find your purpose. According to The Ikigai diagram:

- What the world needs is your mission.

- What you love to do is your passion.

- What you are good at is your profession.

- What you are paid for is your vocation.

- When you connect them all together, you find your purpose.

Developing a blueprint is the next step. This is the third, but most important step. Once you determine who you are and what you love (passion), you need to develop a blueprint to outline your business plan. Be sure to have a vision and mission for your platform. This plan will have short and long-term goals, strategies and activities, financial needs, an executive summary, marketing strategies, and products or services. You can develop a blueprint for anything you want to do.

Once you develop your goals and strategies, you must **monitor the implementation**. You can hire a coach or mentor to help with the accountability. You can also self-monitor. However, managing your time is critical. Select a day of the week to monitor your goals. If you don't meet one of your goals on time or if a strategy was not implemented, look at the root cause and adjust as needed. Journaling is also a great way to document your progress. Write down the lessons learned. When you learn from mistakes, personal growth takes place. Fail forward and celebrate the small wins.

The last step is **networking**. In the social media age, there are so many platforms available and virtual conferences to attend where you can meet like-minded people. I encourage all my clients to network with like minds and surround themselves with positive people. Networking builds relationships, creates opportunities for career growth, and can provide you with access to information that you may need for your business. Sharing digital business cards, friend referrals, attending conferences and speaking engagements are all great ways to network. There are 7.9 billion people in the world. There will always be someone out there who is doing what you want to do. Create your business, hire the right team, and share your gift with the world.

In conclusion, if you trust the process, you will reap the harvest. Farmers follow a process for harvesting crops. The tools must be right, timing is key, the different parts of the plant must be separated, and the crops must be transported and stored properly. Each step is essential in the process. When followed properly there is a bountiful harvest. This is the same for every process including the one mentioned in this chapter. When my clients follow the process, the bountiful harvest is success, fulfillment, prosperity, and inner peace. Once you determine what you are passionate about, you can live in your purpose to help others.

Listed below are tips to use when following any process to reap a harvest:

1.   Concentrate on what you really want to do and stay
        focused on the goal.

2.   Always be persistent and never give up on your dream.

3.   No matter what trials and tribulations come your way,
        embrace the lesson learned and share the lesson with
        someone else.

4.   Embrace the journey and stay grounded in your truth.

You will be successful, fulfilled, prosperous, and have inner peace. Let your light shine and be the best version of you. Follow the process. Reap the harvest.

Her Excellency, Dr. Theresa A. Moseley is originally from Fayetteville, North Carolina. She is a United States Army Veteran, retired educator, motivational speaker, a 16x bestselling author, a 4x international bestselling author, a 3x award-winning educator, and a Word of Life Ministries United Nations Peace Ambassador. She is also a John Maxwell Certified Coach. Dr. Moseley has been featured in several magazines including *International Face*, *Women of Dignity*, *Speakers Magazine*, *Tap-In*, *Vision and Purpose Magazine*, *The Black Family*, and *Called2Inspire Magazine*. Last but not least, she is the Owner/CEO of TAM Creating Ambassadors of Peace.

REFLECTION PAGE

How did the author's story resonate with you? How did the story encourage you? Do you feel that you can execute the tips shared while trusting the process to reap an overwhelmingly successful harvest? Explain below.

REFLECTION PAGE

FAITH/RESILIENCY

According to Merriam-Webster faith means the following: (1) belief and trust in and loyalty to God, (2) complete trust. Resilience is the ability to spring back or bounce back into shape after being bent, or stretched out of the original shape or form. The next four authors have exercised faith and resilience after being stretched and challenged in various ways. Listed below are some of their favorite faith and resilience scriptures.

Now faith is the substance of things hoped for, the evidence of things not seen. (Hebrews 11:1 KJV)

For a just man falleth seven times, and riseth up again: but the wicked shall fall into mischief. (Proverbs 24:16 KJV)

But they that wait upon the LORD shall renew their strength; they shall mount up with wings as eagles; they shall run, and not be weary; and they shall walk, and not faint. (Isaiah 40:31 KJV)

This poor man cried, and the LORD heard him, and saved him out of all his troubles. (Psalm 34:6 KJV)

FAITH

It is impossible to trust the process without exercising faith. Though we may not see the expected harvest we must believe that as we continue to move through the process with faith in God it will manifest. It is no accident that God deliberately wrote the same scripture "the just shall live by faith" in three different places in the Bible. In fact, it sounds like God wants to ensure that we get this very important message about faith. Hebrews 11:6 says, "Without faith, it is impossible to please God."

THE JUST SHALL LIVE BY FAITH. (Romans 1:17 KJV)

BUT THE JUST SHALL LIVE BY HIS FAITH. (Habakkuk 2:4 KJV)

BUT THE JUST SHALL LIVE BY FAITH. (Hebrews 10:38 KJV)

Seize The Moment: Trust the Process

MICHELLE HAMMOND

Throughout my life, trusting the faith process has been tested through various trials. With each one, I gained so much strength. Walk with me as I share my story about the importance of trusting the faith process, its impact on individuals and communities, and how it can be cultivated and maintained in the face of uncertainty, doubt, and adversity. For me, the core process of faith involves placing trust and confidence in someone greater than myself. That someone greater is my Lord and Savior Jesus Christ. This is an act of surrender. I will admit, that it can be both challenging and liberating, as it requires you to let go of your need for certainty and security, and instead, embrace the unknown and the mysterious. One of my aspects of trusting the faith process is the acceptance of uncertainty. In a world that is often characterized by rapid change and unpredictability, faith provides a sense of grounding and stability. This foundation has enabled me to navigate life's challenges and adversities with resilience and hope. I trusted God while experiencing homelessness. He showed up with favors, including sending a social worker to secure housing. Trust the process and know that you can find solace in knowing that a larger plan is at work, though the immediate path ahead seems unclear.

Trusting the faith process has profound implications for personal growth and transformation. When we embrace faith, we open ourselves to new possibilities and experiences, and we become more receptive to guidance and wisdom from unexpected sources. Do you believe that sometimes those unexpected individuals we encounter at the direst times are guided angels? I recall being in certain situations and a stranger would often say something that sparked my interconnectedness. As an example, I may have just recently thought of the same idea or topic this stranger had discussed in this conversation a day or week prior. This revelation brings the openness that allows for a deepening of one's spirituality, a broadening of one's perspective to be attuned, and the potential for transcendence and enlightenment; thus, the mirrored solution of trusting the process.

Consistently trusting the process has not only worked for me, but it has worked in my community. And it has provided a sense of solidarity among many. You may be asking "How can this be?" I am glad you asked. When individuals come together in faith and trust, they form bonds of mutual support and understanding, and they create a space where values such as compassion, empathy, and love can flourish. This typical sense of belonging and interconnectedness has been attributed to placing me in rooms where many have asked "How did you get there?" My response was simply, "I trusted the process." In doing so, I was awarded numerous local community awards including the 2016 Talbot County NAACP Dorothy Black Community Award, the 2021 Changing The Tide Award, and many more. The latest award that I have received was the Governor's Citation from Maryland's first African American Governor Wes Moore. I also hold an appointed position as a board member on Maryland's Health Commission by previous Governor Larry Hogan. It has been the work of creating a community of change while authentically reaching individuals. Admittedly, I recall earlier in life the many naysayers who said negative things and thought that they would deter my focus and destiny. They said that I would never achieve my accomplishments. Well, it looks like they were wrong! Focusing on my goals, I trusted the process and reaped overwhelmingly abundant harvests.

Just remember that some seeds that are being planted for you need nourishment, but let the overflow of God's watering system increase your trust level. There are no promises that this journey will be easy. And for us that can be a bonus learning tool. While I was trusting the process faith sustained me, and character was built.

If this journey is too easy, how will you know to rely on trust? Trusting the faith process is not void of challenges. Doubt, skepticism, and disillusionment can threaten to undermine one's faith and erode the foundations of trust that have been cultivated. In the face of these obstacles, we must draw on our inner resources and community support to reaffirm our commitment to the faith process, even when it feels difficult or uneasy. Now stop and think, "Who in my community can I call on in times like these?" To cultivate and maintain trust in the process which requires faith, individuals can engage in practices that nourish their spiritual well-being and deepen their connection to their beliefs. When I need additional intuition for a project that I am working on, I use the mechanism of sound therapy by using crystal sound bowls with a frequency of 528Hz which heightens creativity. I also use prayer, meditation, contemplation, and acts of service that promote a sense of purpose and meaning as a professional Clinical Mental Health Counselor (CMHC), and just the ordinary person who loves people. I engage in conversations using meaningful dialogue with those I encounter. This requires trusting the process. The valuable reassurance, as well as the opportunity to share and learn from each other's experiences, can be beneficial. Trusting the faith process is a profound and transformative journey that offers individuals the opportunity to relinquish control, embrace uncertainty, and cultivate a deep sense of trust in a higher level of a deity that is greater than themselves. I repeat … greater than themselves. By doing so you can find comfort and resilience in the face of challenges.

Here are a few tips on how to embrace your journey of trusting the process.

1. **Cultivate Self–awareness** – Take time to reflect on your own values, beliefs, and experiences. Understanding oneself and what one truly believes provides a solid foundation for trusting the faith process.

2. **Seek Support** – Connect with a supportive and understanding community. Share experiences and seek guidance from others who share similar beliefs.

3. **Practice Mindfulness** – Engage in practices such as meditation, prayer, or other activities that can help you stay present, focused, and connected to your spiritual beliefs.

4. **Educate Yourself** – Deepen your understanding of your faith by engaging in meaningful dialogue. We must avoid conversations that will hinder our process. Engage in reading sacred texts that can enhance your ability to diminish distractions.

5. **Embrace Uncertainty** – Recognize that this is a natural process and is part of the journey of faith. Embracing these feelings and seeing them as growth opportunities can help strengthen your faith in the process.

6. **Reflect on past experiences** – Recall the times when you relied on your faith to guide you through challenging times or provide clarity and strength. Drawing on these past experiences can reinforce your trust in the faith process.

Incorporating these tips into your daily life can help you nurture and strengthen your trust in the faith process, even when the outlook seems uncertain.

Michelle Hammond is a multi-talented woman who uses her God-given talents to help others. She is also a gifted singer, songwriter, counselor, international bestselling author, podcast host, and small business owner. She is on a mission to flood the world with positivity. She can be found on her weekly podcast, *Upfront: Mind Body Soul - The Trilogy of Wellness*. She has won several awards for her outstanding community service. She is currently a professor for Holistic Professional of Color University and MD Chapter President for Holistic Professional of Color Association.

REFLECTION PAGE

How did the author's story resonate with you? How did the story encourage you? Do you feel that you can execute the tips shared while trusting the process to reap an overwhelmingly successful harvest? Explain below.

REFLECTION PAGE

Faith Amidst Failure: A Story of Academic Resilience

NICOLE GWANZURA

Connecting with others and finding the silver lining has always been my forte. However, falling flat on my face and admitting defeat, especially to those closest to me, has never been easy. I remember distinctly the anxiety of potentially receiving a "C" in graduate school, a grade that threatened to shatter the image of the "golden girl" I was perceived to be. Growing up in Zimbabwe, I never wanted anything. I was a good student and had good friends, and my parents provided all we could want for my siblings and me. Yes, I would have pre-teen angst and squabbles, but I was OK at the end of the day. However, life took a significant turn when, 20 years ago, we embarked on a new journey to the United States, a country that was soon to become our new home. I vividly remember our arrival day as if it were yesterday. My dad had flown in a few weeks earlier to scope out a place to live; my mom had sent him specific instructions for housing within her preferred school district. In the meantime, the rest of the family went on vacation, including going to the beach for the first time. By the way, this was nothing like the America I had seen on TV. Adapting to this new chapter in my life was a testament to my belief in God's plan and my ability to embrace change and I didn't even realize it at the time. Unknowingly, I was already trusting His process.

Fast forward six years later, and I was fresh out of undergrad school, marketing degree in hand, and had decided that there was more to my life than a starter sales job. I spoke with my family and applied to a Business and Corporate Communications program at my alma mater. The MBA program admitted me, but the Communications program I applied to did not. So deciding what to study was easy from there. I knew I could go to school debt-free if

I landed a Resident Director position. The employment would cover my tuition, housing, and fees. Given my experience as a Resident Assistant during undergrad and the good reputation and relationships I had formed, I decided to apply for the role. The interviews were a resounding success! I was so excited; everything was working out as I had planned, and nothing could go wrong, right? Wrong! Everything was great until my class assignments came in. Marketing (yesss!!!), Accounting (manageable…maybe), Economics (absolutely not!). During the first few weeks of school, I was doing my best to manage the program and my work. I made a good friend during the program's first week; my now husband was in the program with me, so I was in good company. I felt comfortable because I also knew the campus and what to expect. The first signs of trouble surfaced when the first Economics exam came around, and more than half the class left the exam room in tears or with long and defeated faces. Even I, the forever optimist, could see the red flags. I continued to put forth my best effort, formed study groups, and revised my work more frequently. I even went to see my economics professor for help, and his exact response was, "Come on, this is so easy my eight-year-old could do it." Needless to say, I knew he would no longer be a helpful resource. Accounting honestly wasn't going that great either, but I was doing my best. I've never been great at math, but at least it wouldn't be as bad as economics.

Fast forward to the end of the first semester, I checked my final grades. I landed an 'A' in Marketing and a 'C' in Economics (surprise, surprise). My accounting professor was so gracious to email me ahead of time after final exams to let me know that my grade would be a 'C.' At that moment, my fate in the program was sealed…or seemingly it was. It was like the world stopped completely, and I was frozen in a nightmare come to life. My program had three 'Cs' and you're OUT policy. I now had to reach out to my boss and share the news that I wasn't going to meet the GPA requirements to stay in the job. I then called my boyfriend and two other close friends on campus. A few hours later, I officially lost my job as Resident Director and needed to vacate the apartment soon after. What happened next was a mix of grace, favor, and mercy I never would've expected amidst impending turmoil.

I called my dad to break the news, and it was hard for him to hear, but he didn't yell or shame me. He was empathetic and practical. I called an apartment complex that happened to have one last basement apartment available. Dad agreed to help me pay rent for the next semester so I could stay in school. Here I was, the first person in my family to attend college and graduate from school in the United States, a well-known student on campus turned immediate "failure." The shame and despair I felt was harrowing. By the end of that weekend, my friends had helped me pack up the apartment and moved me across the street to my new residence. I had to start over as I didn't even have furniture. However, the way that people poured into me was something only God could've orchestrated.

One month later, with the help of my parents, my boyfriend, and student loans, I was back on campus and starting the second semester of my MBA program, and no one outside of my friends knew about the disaster that had occurred. Or so I thought. I later discovered that one of my classmates had replaced me as Resident Director and shared my business with a few other students behind my back. Regardless of the shame he tried to bring upon me, it did not stop me from persevering. I completed that next semester with flying colors. I strategically chose summer school for my next weakest subject, finance, to avoid further academic pitfalls. This decision, guided by faith and practicality, paid off, and I emerged stronger and more accomplished that year. The following Fall marked one year from the day I almost failed, and I finished my coursework confidently and was set to graduate early. However, this didn't stop me from checking my final grades while waiting for the graduation processional to begin. A few minutes later, I was walking across the graduation stage, my favorite professor hooded me, and I heard my family and friends cheer loudly for me. That was it; **I was DONE!** The Lord had seen me through. The plans I had for myself didn't work, but through Him, I could do ALL things because He strengthened me.

It's been 10 years since those challenging times in graduate school, yet the lessons learned remain a pivotal part of my life. Just a few months ago, I found myself back on the familiar stage of my alma mater. However, I wasn't the cautious graduate student tentatively celebrating my success this time. Instead, I stood there confidently as a proud representative of the Alumni Board of Directors, introducing the University President. This moment was a powerful testament to how far I had come, not just in my career but in my personal growth and faith journey. As you reflect on my story, I hope that it resonates with you and provides a roadmap for navigating life's challenges. Here are a few tips I executed while trusting the process to reap an abundantly successful harvest:

1.   **Leverage Every Challenge:** Remember, life's challenges are hidden opportunities. Whether it's turning lemons into a feast or finding the silver lining in tough situations, extracting value from every experience is crucial.

2.   **There's Resilience in Adversity**: Tough times are inevitable, but how we face them shapes our character. Keeping faith and treading lightly through storms allows us to find our footing again.

3.   **Have Faith in the Journey:** Every hardship is a stitch in the fabric of our life story. Trust in God's intentionality and the purpose behind each challenge. In closing, I encourage you to embrace your challenges with faith and resilience.

Each difficulty, from a disheartening grade to moments of doubt, is part of a purposeful journey. Engage with these experiences to grow stronger and wiser. Remember, the process itself enriches your journey. Let it guide you to triumph and personal fulfillment, crafting a story of perseverance and growth. May your path, though winding, lead you to proud achievements and profound self-discovery.

Nicole Gwanzura, MBA, is not only the CEO of Education Advancement Consulting LLC (EAC) but is also a dedicated mother, wife, and believer. As a visionary career strategist, she brings over a decade of transformative impact to early career development and higher education. Her journey as a bilingual immigrant and first-generation college graduate from Zimbabwe enriches her work with unparalleled authenticity and empathy. She is passionate about empowering students and early career professionals through her innovative Career Wellness workshops and personalized programs, charting their courses toward successful careers and academic achievements. As an alumna of Radford University with a bachelor's degree in marketing and an MBA, she proudly serves on Radford's Alumni Board of Directors. Her thought leadership is featured in publications such as *Fortune*, *Her Campus*, and *Poets & Quants*.

REFLECTION PAGE

How did the author's story resonate with you? How did the story encourage you? Do you feel that you can execute the tips shared while trusting the process to reap an overwhelmingly successful harvest? Explain below.

REFLECTION PAGE

Rejection: God's Protection

LaTrish Thomas

Have you ever struggled with rejection? I believe we all have at some point in time. It can be very painful, especially when it comes from someone we love or something we really want. The disappointment of not getting what we thought we wanted, needed, or deserved can leave us questioning ourselves: Are we worthy? Are we capable? Are we deserving? Are we attractive? Are we good enough? The hurt of not being accepted, appreciated, respected, chosen, or loved goes deep. Rejection can leave scars on our hearts that we carry around for a very long time, impacting how we interact with others, make decisions, and show up in the world. Past rejection can be debilitating to our personal and professional growth, and even negatively impact our relationships with others. We become more skeptical, lose hope, are critical of ourselves, and are fearful of taking a chance on the next opportunity.

My personal journey with rejection began very early in my childhood and continued into my teenage years. It mostly stemmed from not feeling seen or accepted. I was very insecure, lacked confidence, and never considered myself the pretty, popular, or talented one. I participated in some activities, did well in school, engaged in church programs, and had a decent number of friends. However, I would not do anything beyond my comfort zone. If I did not fit in naturally, I did not force it. Oftentimes, I would be labeled scary, goody two shoes, teacher's pet, and daddy's girl. But that did not bother me. I always managed to find contentment in doing what was right and true to me, even if that meant being labeled and alone. This mentally helped me in my teenage years to avoid unnecessary trouble and into my young adult years as I began to navigate life. However, growing up it did not always feel good to be left out for choosing not to follow the crowd.

Shortly after I graduated from high school, I joined the military. I had not planned to do so; it was a very spontaneous and ideal decision (that I realized was really God's plan) since I was disciplined, followed the rules, and was a leader at heart. Adjusting to the military was not difficult for me at all. My father had not served in the military but reared my siblings and I in a very militant manner. The hardest part, however, was keeping my mouth closed. I have always spoken my truth and stood up for what was right. That was not the most favorable behavior in an institution that teaches its own code of conduct (do what you are told, don't question your senior leaders, etc.). Because I considered myself a disciplined person, I began to work on myself, particularly my mouth, by studying scriptures that pertain to constraint and being wise with my words. I believed my boldness in speech was a gift and like most gifts and talents, they require sharpening. I did so through the word of God, meditating on scriptures like,

Proverbs 10:19: When there are many words, sin is unavoidable, but the one who controls his lips is wise. (CSB)

James 1:19-20: My dear brothers and sisters, take note of this: Everyone should be quick to listen, slow to speak, and slow to become angry. (NIV)

Proverbs 21:23: Watch your tongue and keep your mouth shut, and you will stay out of trouble. (NLT)

These are a few of the scriptures I used that began to sharpen my communication skills and improved how I voiced my concerns. I did not know it at the time, but I was prepared to fulfill my purpose in my career, ministry, and life. As I began to control my tongue, more opportunities became available to me. Leaders quickly chose me because I did not follow the crowd, I spoke with conviction and integrity, I was trusted, and although I was not always confident in myself, I knew how to be my most authentic self.

I digress to share about the area of communication I had to work on because it is a crucial part of my journey of rejection and God's protection. Both were a gift from Him. Once I realized that not everyone is for me and not everything is for me to react to, I began to respond to rejection differently.

I have encountered some very painful and disappointing situations that I had to move past because I trusted God and believed He knew what was best. There was a time when I questioned God why He did or did not allow certain things to happen. I also felt I had to question or challenge the person who rejected me. I needed answers! I needed clarity! This can't be right! This isn't fair! However, the biggest lesson was that not every rejection required a response from me nor a justification from God and the other person. Also, I realized every rejection created an opportunity to gain experience and to grow. Both lessons required me to be still (be quiet) and trust that He is God. Those two things are what shaped the character needed to go through the process and continuously reap the rewards God had prepared for me. In Isaiah 30:15, the Lord said, "In quietness and trust is your strength."

All throughout my life, in every assignment, every tough decision, every heartbreak, every denial of promotion, every rejection from friends and loved ones, every setback and failure, every mistreatment and defamation of character, every failed relationship, every uncomfortable encounter, I have been able to overcome gracefully by the strength of God that was developed through quietness and trust.

The strategic steps I took to master rejection as protection were to first be comfortable with being my authentic self by not allowing the world or situations to change who I was but allowing the Word of God to change me. I then realized, like each of you, I am uniquely different and flawed so I learned to meet people where they are, extend grace, and allow space for growth and change. I continuously strengthened my gifts and skills which separated me from the crowd and prepared me for the next season of my life. I became wise with my words; not seeing silence as defeat but as a moment to hear from God saying how he would have me to respond. Lastly, I stopped using rejection as a tool to measure myself negatively and used it as an opportunity to see what God is showing and teaching me, preparing me for, or letting me know that better is coming.

When I began to welcome rejection as God's protection, I also allowed the stumbling blocks to become my stepping stones. Rejection serves as a redirection; a closed door can create opportunities for new doors to open that we would not have discovered if it weren't for the "no" we received. Also, during times of what felt like isolation, I was able to spend more time in prayer, Bible study, community service, and personal development. As I continued to move forward, it built my confidence, improved my character, increased my faith, and most importantly, strengthened my trust in God. I became more dependent on Him, His word, and my relationship with Him. My life became better and my purpose clearer. I am now operating in the calling God had for my life: to teach others how to live fully and authentically, to advocate for diversity and inclusion, and to spread the Word of God.

Your situation may not be ideal right now, however, remain focused and trust the process that will lead you to an overwhelmingly successful harvest. The following are tips to help you stay the course while trusting the process en route to achieving your overwhelmingly successful harvest:

• Be your authentic self because everyone else is taken. Your uniqueness becomes your secret sauce that others cannot easily replicate or duplicate.

• Stay on the Potter's wheel and let the Word of God continuously mold you. He is the sovereign creator with the authority to make and mold you until he sees himself in you. In essence, no one knows its product better than the creator/inventor.

• Operate in your gifts and continue to refine them because this is where you will experience grace and strength for the journey. Stay in your lane serving your God ordained gifts with excellence.

• Accept rejection as an opportunity to grow, or as God's sign of redirection to something better.

LaTrish Thomas is a minister and human services professional with a passion for serving God and serving people. She is the owner of Affirmed Life Fitness, LLC where she encourages others to live a healthy and balanced life with JOY and GRATITUDE; she incorporates faith, health, and finding contentment in life. LaTrish served 21 years in the United States Army and now serves as a Crisis Responder in the area of suicide prevention. She holds a master's degree in human services with a concentration in Counseling. She spends her free time traveling, being with family, doing outdoor activities, or attending the performing arts.

REFLECTION PAGE

How did the author's story resonate with you? How did the story encourage you? Do you feel that you can execute the tips shared while trusting the process to reap an overwhelmingly successful harvest? Explain below.

REFLECTION PAGE

Harvest of Resilience: Trusting Life's Process and Embracing Second Chances

DR. TALVIA PETERSON

As I reflect on the journey that has brought me to this moment, it gives me an even deeper appreciation and love for my parents. In life, trusting the process was a lesson I have learned with each passing season in my life. My home whispered lessons of resilience, faith, trust, and the unwavering belief in trusting the process that has led me to a bountiful harvest.

My beginnings run deep, not just into the soil of my family, but into the profound experiences that have shaped me. My dad, a seasoned veteran of the United States Marine Corps, instilled in me the values of emotional management, discipline, and commitment, while my mom's motherly and medical wisdom provided a unique perspective on the importance of faith, patience, and trust in the process.

In the early days of my life, life had thrown unexpected challenges my way, and there were moments when trusting the process meant trusting the very essence of my life itself. As I gained strength from hearing the heartache, faith, and love DURING the time my heart stopped beating, not once, but twice. This dramatic ordeal tested not only my physical strength but also the collective strength and faith of my family. Gasping for air as my aunt carried me in her arms while running down the street to meet the ambulance that rushed me to the hospital. All of the doors to the house were wide open, and all of the lights were left on as my working parents received a phone call from someone who said, "We have taken Talvia to the hospital due to a severe seizure and her heart has flatlined." My parents, drawing on the lessons of Marine and medical professionals, had to lean on each other and trust in the process of medical intervention and the innate resilience of the human spirit.

"It was never an option that we would lose Talvia," said my father. As my family battled through what appeared to be the darkest of these moments, my parents clung to hope and trusted in the expertise of a host of specialists. There was a time when my parents' education and careers were once the center of their world. But that took a backseat to the urgency of my survival. The heart that had beat to the rhythm of energy and joy was now fighting for its own existence.

The echoes of my dad saying, "Adapt and overcome" or "As long as she is crying, she's okay" and my mom's patience and perseverance as she leaned on my dad when not seeing the solution, became not just guiding principles for my life, but lifelines during those critical hours. Trusting the process of the medical personnel, while having seizure after seizure, was a true mark of having faith in the resilience of the human body and embracing the uncertainty of the journey. These were not just theoretical concepts; they were the anchors that kept me tethered to life itself.

And just as the medicine was working and another level of faith was achieved, the second phone call came in saying that I had another severe seizure and the school rushed me to the hospital. Imagine being told that your child's heart stopped beating again but he or she is a fighter, he or she is strong. Surviving that distressing and heartbreaking experience became a testament to the connection of my work ethic, a commitment to constantly improve, and exhibiting unwavering gratefulness each day. It was as if the very essence of flatlining, not once but twice, mirrored the resilience that my family and I with the medical team had shown in the face of adversity.

As seasons changed, our wisdom and faith grew and so did I. The once unhealthy young girl transformed into a resilient steward of gratitude and faith, armed with the discipline of a Marine, the nurturing heart and unbelievable belief of a mother and close aunt, and the profound gratitude for the gift of a second chance at life. Each setback at the hospital became a reminder of the fragility of existence, and every harvest was a celebration of life's resilience.

As the first signs of a seizure-free life appeared, my family and I marveled at the harmonization and progression of faith. It is a constant reminder that our dreams and endeavors need time to mature. Trusting the process meant appreciating the small victories along the way – the heartbeat after flatlining, the fever dropping, and the signs of progress that might go unnoticed. The satisfaction and gratefulness I felt were not just from the abundance and strength of my heartbeat, but knowing that my family and I embraced the challenges and tapped into each other's strengths; we remained true to the mission and allowed the process to unfold with little evidence.

In life, the journey is as important as the destination. Trusting the process is never a guarantee of life, but rather it is a commitment to faith and perseverance, a recognition that setbacks are part of the narrative and that every season of life contributes to the eventual harvest. As I close my eyes, I am grateful for the strength to fight and overcome challenges, the lessons learned, and the wisdom gained by trusting the process.

Here are three specific tips and lessons learned that will enable you to trust the process and reap an abundantly fulfilling harvest:

1.   **Embrace Patience and Persistence:** Trusting the process requires a steadfast commitment to both patience and persistence. Just as an entrepreneur doesn't always see immediate results, recognize that personal and professional growth takes time. Be patient with yourself and enjoy the journey, understanding that setbacks are part of the process. Persistence ensures that you continue to put in the effort consistently, learn from experiences,

and navigate challenges with calmness and resilience. Remember, a bountiful harvest is often the result of steady faith and dedication.

2.   **Gradual Progress and Trust:** Instead of aiming for immediate, major leaps, gradual progress involves celebrating small milestones that allow you to track progress and gain trust along the way. This not only boosts your confidence but also reinforces that each day of gratefulness and each win contributes to the overall success of your outcome. Trusting the process becomes more evident when you can journal and measure your advancements and witness the gradual transformation of your efforts into meaningful outcomes.

3.   **Cultivate a Faith-Filled Positive Mindset:** A growing faith and a positive mindset are both powerful tools in trusting the process. Cultivate an environment of positivity and support that focuses on the opportunities presented by challenges rather than dwelling on the obstacles. Embrace a growth mindset that sees setbacks as opportunities to go around, jump over, and push through to improvement. Surround yourself with a supportive community that lifts you up, makes you stronger, encourages your journey, and shares in your vision. By journaling your manifestation of gratitude daily and striving to maintain a positive outlook, you will not only alleviate the stress of negativity but also create an environment conducive to reaping a more abundant and fulfilling harvest in various areas of your life.

Remember, the process is not just about the destination; it's about the transformative journey that shapes you into the woman or man along the way. Harvesting resilience and trusting in the process, while executing these tips and practical life lessons, will pave the way for a more resilient, purposeful journey, as you consistently embrace opportunities to live a successful life and reap overwhelmingly successful harvests.

Dr. Talvia Peterson is the CEO and Founder of A Pink Success, LLC, and Sole Proprietor/Owner of Here to Serve Realty. She is an accomplished author of *Never Do Average: A 5-Minute Inspirational Gratitude Journal* and Co-Author of the highly anticipated International Bestseller Anthology titled *Trust the Process – Reap the Harvest*. She was recently awarded the RRAR Committee Chairperson of the Year Award, the Property Empire Builder Award, the Presidential Lifetime Achievement Award, and The 44th Presidential Legacy Lifetime Achievement Award. She led a team of women to recognize April 10, 2009, officially as 100 Black Women Empowerment Day at the state capitol in Georgia (House Resolution 913), titled "A United Voice for Change – A Day of Empowerment and Motivation."

REFLECTION PAGE

How did the author's story resonate with you? How did the story encourage you? Do you feel that you can execute the tips shared while trusting the process to reap an overwhelmingly successful harvest? Explain below.

REFLECTION PAGE

TRUST YOUR PILOT— EPILOGUE

DON'T ALLOW ANYONE OR ANYTHING TO DETER YOUR FOCUS

You must trust your pilot. After all, he has your flight plan, and he's well able to ensure that you safely reach your destination. He even knows the way through the wilderness. And since he is your creator and the creator of the universe, there is no risk of him getting lost or leading you to the wrong place. Ponder that thought for a moment. In fact, Psalm 139:7 asks, "Whither shall I go from thy spirit? or whither shall I flee from thy presence?" And Psalm 139:8-16 substantiates the fact that we cannot hide from our pilot. We are always on his radar. That is why we can trust the process because we are never alone.

[8] If I ascend up into heaven, thou art there: if I make my bed in hell, behold, thou art there.

[9] If I take the wings of the morning, and dwell in the uttermost parts of the sea;

[10] Even there shall thy hand lead me, and thy right hand shall hold me.

[11] If I say, Surely the darkness shall cover me; even the night shall be light about me.

[12] Yea, the darkness hideth not from thee; but the night shineth as the day: the darkness and the light are both alike to thee.

[13] For thou hast possessed my reins: thou hast covered me in my mother's womb.

[14] I will praise thee; for I am fearfully and wonderfully made: marvelous are thy works; and that my soul knoweth right well.

[15] My substance was not hid from thee, when I was made in secret, and curiously wrought in the lowest parts of the earth.

[16] Thine eyes did see my substance, yet being unperfect; and in thy book all my members were written, which in continuance were fashioned, when as yet there was none of them.

Our pilot is a part of the control tower and does not have to wait for instructions to take off or land. He is in charge. He never needs to refuel the plane; he doesn't have to update his navigation system. He is Omnipresent, Omniscient and Omnipotent. WOW! Show me someone who can top that. With those amazing credentials, we surely can trust our pilot. Step by step, we can learn to trust him more each day. And as we trust him more, that involves trusting his process.

One of the authors shared her amazingly compelling story about being challenged during her flight. Eventually, she realized that she needed to release the anxiety and the other emotions that deterred her focus. At the end of the day, she arrived at her destination safe and sound. And it is my prayer that you will have the same testimony. So, trust the process, realizing that your pilot knows every step you need to safely arrive at your destination. When your path seemingly gets dark, trust the process because your pilot is the light of the world, and he promised to never leave you nor forsake you. And he is faster than a 747 jumbo jet. He promised to be at your beckoning call before you can say His name according to Isaiah 65:24 "And it shall come to pass, that before they call, I will answer; and while they are yet speaking, I will hear."

And remember that you have present confidence based on past experience. God has delivered us from fiery furnaces on several occasions. He has an impeccable track record that is out of the world. Therefore, we should be able to remember his faithfulness. We should know that he is not a man to lie. If he said it, then it must come to pass. And if that is not enough, remember that He loves us with an everlasting love. What love!

Lastly, remember that our pilot is also our shepherd, and he offers amazing benefits out of this world. Psalm 23 below reminds us of his great care for us.

Psalm 23 (KJV)

¹ The Lord is my Shepherd; I shall not want.

² He maketh me to lie down in green pastures: He leadeth me beside the still waters.

³ He restoreth my soul: He leadeth me in the paths of righteousness for His name's sake.

⁴ Yea, though I walk through the valley of the shadow of death, I will fear no evil: for thou art with me; thy rod and thy staff they comfort me.

⁵ Thou preparest a table before me in the presence of mine enemies: thou anointest my head with oil; my cup runneth over.

⁶ Surely goodness and mercy shall follow me all the days of my life: and I will dwell in the house of the Lord forever.

This has always been one of my Psalms of encouragement. And I would not be surprised if it is yours as well. Allow it to help you trust the process and reap an overwhelmingly abundant harvest. Here is a slightly modified version that can be used as encouraging affirmations.

<u>The Lord *is* my Shepherd, I shall not want</u>. Notice that I didn't say the government or my husband of 50 years, but THE Lord Jesus is my personal shepherd right now **in this present time**. The word "is" denotes the present tense. Because He is my Shepherd, I have a relationship with Him. I can talk with Him throughout the day when I come boldly to the throne of grace. There, I expect to find grace and mercy to help in my very time of need. What a relationship based upon His unconditional love for me. **I shall not want, not Pre-pandemic, during the pandemic, or post-pandemic!** That's overflow because He has promised in Philippians 4:19 to supply my every need one by one as I walk upright in His Word, His Will, and His Way. The Good Shepherd desires that His sheep have only the best. God provides my every need. In fact, He is my source and total resource.

He maketh me to lie down in green pastures—**That's rest**. Have you ever been tired or exhausted? Once you took time to rest you felt so refreshed and revived. That's what our Shepherd does for us. He provides sweet rest especially when we cast our every care upon Him. He is the man for the job, and since He will be up all night anyway, cast your care upon Him, and allow Him to bless you to lie down in green pastures.

He leadeth me beside the still waters—**That's refreshment.** I can recall feeling so refreshed after drinking a cold glass of water on a very hot day. That is what our Shepherd does. He provides refreshments when the need arises.

He restoreth my soul—**That's healing**. All have sinned and come short of the glory of God. But we can confess our sins (I John 1:9), turn from them, and have restored fellowship with God. That fellowship can fill us with incomparable joy and peace. Allow Him to give you new thoughts, and ideas. And of course, He heals us physically. Psalm 107:20 reminds us that He sent His Word and healed us.

He leadeth me in the paths of righteousness—**That's guidance**. Once we accept the Lord Jesus as our Master, Ruler, and Controller, we have a blessed assurance in Psalm 32:8 which states *"I will instruct thee and teach thee in the way which thou shalt go: I will guide thee with mine eye."* Therefore, when we follow Him, we reach our destination safely. You cannot do it alone, but you can do ALL things through Christ who strengthens you daily.

He just doesn't lead us in the path of righteousness, but He does it—<u>For His Namesake</u>—That's purpose. Jeremiah 29:11 says, *"For I know the thoughts that I think toward you, saith the Lord, thoughts of peace, and not of evil, to give you an expected end.* Since He created us, surely, He knows His expectations of us.

<u>**Yea, though I walk through the valley of the shadow of death**</u>**—That's testing.** We all have challenges in life. The Word of God says that many are the afflictions of the righteous, **but the Lord shall deliver Him out of them all**. So, make no mistake about it, we're in a fixed fight but we have been declared the winner by unanimous decision—The Father, The Son, and the Holy Spirit. GLORY!

<u>**I will fear no evil**</u>**—That's protection.** Psalm 91:15 says, *"I will be with him in trouble; I will deliver him, and honor him."* Not only will our Great God deliver us, but He will HONOR us.

<u>**I will not fear, for thou art with me**</u> **— That's faithfulness.** We can count on God because He never reneges on a promise. His Word says, *"God is not a man to lie, if He said it, He is well able to bring it to pass."*

<u>**Thy Rod and thy staff they comfort me**</u> **—That's discipline**. These symbols can be applied to the life of a Christian when considering God's protection and correction in our lives. The verse states, *"Your rod and your staff, they comfort me."* We should find comfort in the fact that our Shepherd (God) protects us from evil. Sometimes it may be more difficult to find comfort in the fact that God corrects us, but if you consider that the shepherd is much smarter than the sheep (God knows more than we will ever know) and knows what dangers lie around the corner, then we should be able to take comfort in the fact that our Shepherd guides us.

<u>**Thou preparest a table before me in the presence of mine enemies**</u> **—That's hope.** In the midst of great trouble, distress, and affliction, in an orderly way, God prepares and organizes a

long table of provision (nothing missing) and sustenance for each of us — for you and for me. When you are going through a time of trouble and distress, remind God what His Word says about taking care of you. Before one jot or title of His Word shall fail, heaven and earth shall pass away.

<u>Thou anointest my head with oil </u>—That's consecration! It is wonderful to be set apart for the Master's use and purpose.

<u>My cup runneth over </u>—THAT'S ABUNDANCE! Not just enough but MORE THAN ENOUGH! **Surely (TRULY/DEFINITELY) goodness and mercy shall follow me all the days of my life —That's a cup overflowing with blessings!**

<u>And I will dwell in the house of the Lord (DEBT FREE) FOREVER </u>—THAT'S SECURITY! GLORY TO GOD! PARDON ME WHILE I SHOUT!

With these wonderful provisions, you can surely keep the faith, and trust the proess that will yield an overwhelmingly successful harvest!!!

CONCLUSION

There are times in our lives when we are uncertain and unsure of our next steps. Whenever that happens, I seek the Lord in prayer, and He always directs my steps as promised in Proverbs 3:5-6: "Trust in the LORD with all thine heart; and lean not unto thine own understanding. In all thy ways acknowledge Him, and he shall direct thy paths." On November 21, 1996, at 11:00 a.m. I recorded a journal entry that read, "Listen to the voice of your Father. Listen closely and you will hear my voice. Follow the path I have designed for thee. Turn neither to the left or right. Continue to trust me and I WILL bring it to pass." And on September 28, 2003, my journal entry read "Continue to trust me and I'll bring it to pass. There is so much I'm doing for you; you can't see it, that's why you MUST trust me."

On two specific occasions, I exercised child-like faith and trusted God's process, knowing that HE had promised to bring it to pass. I, like Abraham, did not know the where, or when but I continued to trust God. Admittedly, this was not always easy. However, step by step, I began to see some of my dreams and visions manifest. Because I trusted God's process, I continued to reap overwhelmingly successful harvests. He has allowed me to meet some of the most amazing humans on Planet Earth. I have been mentored, trained, and certified by some phenomenally impactful global coaches who have poured into me. And I have partnered with globally phenomenally impactful coaches. TO GOD BE ALL THE GLORY! It is very important to trust the process that will lead to an overwhelmingly successful harvest.

I am beyond grateful that I continued to trust the process which allowed me to garner the support of some phenomenal authors and industry experts. It has been my pleasure to introduce them and to share their awesome stories to help you navigate through various life processes. Our stories are about us, but they are not exclusively for us. Therefore, it was not robbery to serve as scribes while globally sharing our stories. Our compelling experiences are meant to encourage and empower others challenged while trusting the process of encountering speed bumps, detours, road closures, and the dead-end signs of life. Speed bumps allow us to slow down in life. While navigating your process, if you find yourself traveling too fast, imagine that you are at a speed bump and slow down so that you can recalibrate your journey. If you come upon a detour sign during your journey, ensure that you take the correct exit that will allow you to get back on track. And don't allow the road closures or dead-end signs to pull you off focus, because sometimes they are needed when we are entertaining negativity. While trusting the process, we may encounter a roadwork ahead sign. Simply proceed with caution and ensure that you remain single-eye-focused on the process. Simply, change the negative mindset, shift gears into overdrive which leads to positivity, and proceed to trust the process.

So, whatever process you find yourself facing today, know that your victory has been factored in from day one. You were born to win, and you are more than a conqueror. Believe in yourself, continue to trust the process, and don't dare attempt to abort. Because when you do, you will rob yourself of an overwhelmingly successful harvest. You will miss the opportunities for growth that include character development, patience, experience, and several important life lessons. Trust the process so that you will be able to share your lessons with those assigned to you during your journey. Allow them to glean hope knowing that you survived the same challenges they're facing. Remember that your story is about you, but it is not for you. Your story allows you to empower, educate, and equip others to press into adversity until stumbling blocks become stepping stones to victory.

Though your process may have seemed long, drawn out, and unobtainable, when you get to the end you will not look like what you've been through. It may have felt like a fiery furnace, but you will not smell like smoke. Lastly, those who may be experiencing a challenging situation or circumstance trust the process. Fasten your seatbelt and prepare for your victorious journey ahead.

HOW TO FIND FULFILLMENT

Finding fulfillment in life is an ever-evolving process. This may not be the easiest thing to do, especially if you find yourself performing several tasks throughout the day. If you are unsure of what you love, ask yourself the following questions:

> If I had a choice of doing one thing for the rest of my life, what would that be?

> What did I enjoy doing in my childhood?

> What activity makes me feel like I am in my zone?

> What am I doing when I feel like I'm in my "sweet spot?"

> What activity do I love so much that I would do it even if I did not get paid?

> What activity provides such a sense of fulfillment until time gets away very quickly because I am enjoying myself?

> What is the one activity I dreamed about, but never acted upon it?

> What is my hobby?

Asking yourself these questions, you'll begin to notice a pattern of repetitive answers forming, indicating what you absolutely love. Look closely at your answers. You will have a starting point to determine what you love. One of the best ways to determine what you love to do is to seek God through prayer and fasting. Since He created you in His image and likeness, surely, He knows exactly what problem He created you to solve before you left His assembly line. Not only does He know the problem He created you to solve, but He also gave you every ingredient that you would need to fulfill your purpose and assignment. Therefore, you can ask Him the specific purpose He had in mind when He created you. As you begin the process of fasting and praying and seeking God for the answer to your specific purpose, you will also notice that you develop a more intimate relationship with Him. You will be more cognizant and alert to His voice when He speaks. Therefore, you will know when He reveals what you were created to do. When God created you, He had a specific purpose in mind.

According to Dr. Myles Munroe, *"God created everything for a purpose and equipped each created thing with the corresponding potential or ability to fulfill that purpose. All of nature testifies to this great truth, as is evidenced by the fact that seeds always carry within themselves the germ of the trees they were destined to produce. In every bird, there is a flock, in every cow a herd, in every fish a school, and in every wolf a pack. Everything is pregnant with the potential to become all it was created to be…"*

<u>**Dr. Myles Munroe says "Purpose is…**</u>

…the original intent for the creation of a thing,

…the original reason for the existence of a thing;

…the end for which the means exist;

…the cause for the creation of a thing;

…the desired result that initiated production;

…the need that makes a manufacturer produce a specific product;

…the destination that prompts the journey;

That explains why millions are walking around every day frustrated and unfulfilled. **Life simply has no meaning for them because they have not discovered their purpose.** Therefore, it is very important to discover one's purpose to help provide the fulfillment God has created each of us to experience.

Remember, God created you and me to solve a specific problem in the earth realm. And until we discover our purpose, we may go through life simply existing and not thriving and experiencing fulfillment. **So, pay close attention to those things that annoy you.** Could that be a part of your purpose? Could it be a problem you were created to solve?

Another method to discovering your purpose that will help you do what you love is to determine your strengths and your weaknesses. This can be determined by your motivational gifts. There are some things that you are just gifted and graced to do. In fact, when you operate in your gifting you operate like a well-oiled machine. Your gift looks so good on you, and it provides a tremendous sense of fulfillment. What is the one thing that you were afraid to attempt because you felt that you would fail? You felt that you were just not good enough to succeed if you attempted it. However, you may have noticed that because you did not step up to the plate to attempt to flow in your gifting, the urge or unction never left you. Deep within you thought about how you could perform only if you were motivated and confident enough. Allow me to share a secret found in Romans 11:29, *"for God's gifts and his call are irrevocable."* (NIV)

Simply put, God placed within you at least one gift to bring Him glory. Just because you were not aware of the gift, or you were afraid to use your gift, He never changed His mind. He waited for you to realize that once you discovered your gift, you would never work another day in your life. You see your gift will make room for you and bring God all the glory. You will not be totally fulfilled unless you are serving your gift in the area where you are assigned. If you are an exhorter, you must encourage others to aspire to reach their goals and feel good about themselves. If you are an apostle, you are honored to help others set up churches like the Apostle Paul did. If you are a teacher, you are quite satisfied teaching God's Word, so that others may apply it to their lives. And, if you are a preacher, you share God's word so that it may be used to change lives daily.

So, after asking yourself what is the one thing that would bring you fulfillment, focus on your answer. Take time to reflect upon your motivational gift(s) as described in Romans 12:6-8 below:

6 We have different gifts, according to the grace given to each of us. If your gift is prophesying, then prophesy in accordance with your faith;

7 if it is serving, then serve; if it is teaching then teach;

8 if it is to encourage, then give encouragement; if it is giving, then give generously; if it is to lead, do it diligently; if it is to show mercy, do it cheerfully. (NIV)

FIND YOUR WHY. What fuels your journey? What provides you energy when you sometimes feel like you cannot take another step? That specific assignment will provide you with the fulfillment to empower and pour into others. You will go to bed thinking about the newfound fulfillment, it will serve as your alarm clock, and you will definitely awaken flowing with passion.

Once you find your tailor-made purpose that brings you fulfillment, it can become almost impossible to separate you from that amazing feeling. You can almost eat, sleep, and serve others daily because you, too, are being fulfilled and you pour into others. It is very important that you stay in your God-assigned lane and continue doing what you love if you plan to remain fulfilled. Your passion, excitement, and joy are a by-product of your fulfillment. However, someone else would be bored, disinterested, and have no tolerance for what you are doing because it is not their purpose/assignment; therefore, it would not be fulfilling to them.

"Success without fulfillment is the ultimate failure."
Tony Robbins

CONFIDENCE FOR THE PROCESS

HOW TO BE MORE CONFIDENT

Don't compare yourself to others; focus on you.

Relax, don't sweat the small stuff.

Love yourself, you are a gift, nothing would be the same if you didn't exist.

Be positive and look for the good in every situation. Don't beat yourself up if you stumble; pick yourself up, dust yourself off, and get back into the race.

DON'T QUIT

Variation of "Don't Quit" original poem by poet,

John Greenleaf Whittier (1807-1892)

When things go wrong, as they sometimes will,
When the road you're trudging seems all uphill,
When the funds are low and the debts are high,
And you want to smile but you have to sigh,
When care is pressing you down a bit—
Rest if you must, but don't you quit.
Life is odd with its twists and turns,
As everyone sometimes learns.
And many a person turns about
When an individual might have won
had he or she stuck it out.
Don't give up though the pace seems slow—
You may succeed with yet another blow.

Often the goal is nearer than it seems
To a faint and faltering woman or man;
Often the struggler has given up
When he or she might have captured the victor's cup;
And one learned too late when the night came down,
How close he or she was to the golden crown.

Success is failure turned inside out—
The silver tint of the clouds of doubt,
And when you never can tell how close you are,
It may be near when it seems afar;
So stick to the fight when you're hardest hit—
It's when things seem worse, that you mustn't quit.